Teaching Practices from America's Best Urban Schools

A Guide for School and Classroom Leaders

Joseph F. Johnson, Jr., Ph.D.
Lynne G. Perez, Ph.D.
Cynthia L. Uline, Ph.D.

Routledge
Taylor & Francis Group

LONDON AND NEW YORK

First Published 2012 by Eye On Education

Published 2013 by Routledge
2 Park Square, Milton Park, Abingdon, Oxon OX14 4RN
711 Third Avenue, New York, NY, 10017, USA

Routledge is an imprint of the Taylor & Francis Group, an informa business

Library of Congress Cataloging-in-Publication Data

Johnson, Joseph F., Jr.
Teaching practices from America's best urban schools : a guide for school and classroom
leaders / Joseph F. Johnson, Jr., Ph.D., Lynne G. Perez, Ph.D., Cynthia L. Uline, Ph.D.
        pages   cm
ISBN 978-1-59667-234-5
1. Education, Urban—United States.
2. Students with social disabilities—United States.
3. Education—Parent participation—United States.
I. Title.
LC5131.J65 2012
370.9173'2--dc23   2012038500

ISBN: 978-1-59667-234-5 (pbk)

Cover Designer: Armen Kojoyian

This book is dedicated
to our nation's greatest hope,
America's urban school teachers.

Contents

About the Authors xi
Acknowledgments xiii
Introduction xv

1 Understanding and Using This Book 1
The Schools We Studied 1
Focus on Teaching Practices 2
How to Use This Book 4
How the Book Is Organized 4

2 Focusing on Mastery 7
Planning for Mastery 8
Objective-Driven Lessons 9
Depth of Understanding 11
Time on Objective 12
Focusing on All Students 13
What It Is & What It Isn't 15
Practice Guide Related to Focusing on Mastery 19
Suggested Readings Related to Focusing on Mastery 20

3 Introducing Content Logically, Clearly, and Concisely 23
Logical Introduction of Content, One Step at a Time 24
Clarity Is a Virtue 26
Concise Presentations 27
What It Is & What It Isn't 29
Practice Guide Related to Introducing Content Logically,
      Clearly, and Concisely 32
Suggested Readings Related to Introducing Content Logically,
      Clearly, and Concisely 33

4 Acquiring and Responding to Evidence of Understanding 37
Frequency of Checking for Understanding 38
Well-Distributed Checking for Understanding 40
Checking for Higher Levels of Understanding 42
Observing and Adapting 43
Adequate Daily Progress for Every Student 44
What It Is & What It Isn't 45

Practice Guide Related to Acquiring and Responding
   to Evidence of Understanding 47
Suggested Readings Related to Acquiring and Responding
   to Evidence of Understanding 49

5 **Connecting with Student Interests, Backgrounds, Cultures,
   and Prior Knowledge**... 53
   Building Connections 54
   Not Simply for the Sake of "Interesting"......................... 55
   Assumption of Student Ability 56
   Ongoing Checking to Ensure Connection 57
   What It Is & What It Isn't 58
   Practice Guide Related to Connecting with Student Interests,
      Backgrounds, Cultures, and Prior Knowledge................ 60
   Suggested Readings Related to Connecting with Student
      Interests, Backgrounds, Cultures, and Prior Knowledge 60

6 **Building Student Vocabulary**................................. 63
   Pre-Identification of Critical Vocabulary 64
   Building "Ownership" of Critical Vocabulary 65
   Usable Word Walls 67
   Original Writing... 67
   What It Is & What It Isn't 68
   Practice Guide Related to Building Student Vocabulary........... 70
   Suggested Readings Related to Building Student Vocabulary 71

7 **Promoting Successful Practice**.............................. 75
   Guided Practice 77
   Guided Struggle... 78
   Monitoring Independent Work 79
   Building Student Capacity to Self-Monitor 79
   Providing Independent Work (Including Homework)
      Worth Completing 80
   What It Is & What It Isn't 81
   Practice Guide Related to Promoting Successful Practice.......... 85
   Suggested Readings Related to Promoting Successful Practice 86

8 **Making Students Feel Valued and Capable** 89
   Caring Enough to Demand the Best........................... 90
   Caring Enough to Ensure Success............................. 91
   Caring Enough to Know and Value Individual Students 92
   Caring Enough to Model Courtesy and Respect 93
   Caring Enough to Praise and Acknowledge 94
   Caring Enough to Create Attractive Physical Environments 95
   What It Is & What It Isn't 95

Practice Guide Related to Making Students Feel Valued
and Capable 100
Suggested Readings Related to Making Students Feel Valued
and Capable 100

9 Leading Students to Love Learning 105
Enthusiastic Teaching 107
Relevance of the Content 107
Integration of the Arts, Technology, and Physical Education 108
Student-to-Student Engagement 110
What It Is & What It Isn't 110
Practice Guide Related to Leading Students to Love Learning 113
Suggested Readings Related to Leading Students
to Love Learning 114

10 Developing Best Practices Throughout a School 119
Challenge 1: People are not likely to change their practice
if they don't believe the change will generate worthwhile
learning results for their students. 120
Challenge 2: People are not likely to change their practice
if they believe they already implement the requested
change. 121
Challenge 3: People are not likely to change their practice
if they perceive that nobody cares or notices if they
endeavor to change. 122
Challenge 4: People are not likely to change their practice
if they perceive they are being asked to change multiple
things simultaneously. 123
Challenge 5: People are not likely to change their practice
if they perceive that they are likely to fail when they try. 123
Challenge 6: People are not likely to change their practice
if they perceive they do not have the resources, materials,
time, training, or support necessary to implement the
change successfully. 124
Challenge 7: People find it hard to persist. 125

Conclusion 127

*Appendix A: National Excellence in Urban Education
2013 Eligibility Criteria* 129
*Appendix B: National Excellence in Urban Education
Award Winners* 135
References 141

About the Authors

Joseph F. Johnson, Jr., Ph.D., is the Executive Director of the National Center for Urban School Transformation and the Qualcomm Professor of Urban Education within the Department of Educational Leadership at San Diego State University. He has previously served as a teacher, school and district administrator, state education agency administrator in Texas and Ohio, researcher and technical assistance provider, and U.S. Department of Education official. His research focuses upon schools that achieve remarkable academic results for diverse populations of students. His work has appeared in journals such as *Education and Urban Society*, *Educational Administration Quarterly*, *Educational Leadership*, *International Journal of Leadership in Education*, *Journal of Education for Students Placed at Risk*, *Phi Delta Kappan*, and *Theory into Practice*.

Lynne G. Perez, Ph.D., is the Associate Director of the National Center for Urban School Transformation at San Diego State University. She also serves as a part-time lecturer with San Diego State's Department of Educational Leadership. She serves as an executive coach in the center's Advancing Principal Leadership in Urban Schools Program. Her work on school leadership issues has appeared in journals such as *Educational Administration Quarterly*, *Educational Leadership*, *Journal of Education for Students Placed at Risk*, *Journal of Educational Leadership*, *Journal of School Leadership*, and *Teacher College Record*.

Cynthia L. Uline, Ph.D., is a professor of educational leadership at San Diego State University and executive director of San Diego State's National Center for the 21st Century Schoolhouse: coe.sdsu.edu/edl/schoolhouse/index.php. She also served as an assistant and associate professor of educational administration at The Ohio State University from 1995 to 2005. Her research explores the influence of built learning environments on students' learning, as well as the roles educational leaders, teachers, and the community play in shaping these learning spaces. Other areas of research include school leadership for learning and school reform and improvement. Her work has appeared in journals such as *Educational Administration Quarterly*, *Journal of Educational Administration*, *Teachers College Record*, *Journal of School Leadership*, *Journal of Education for Students Placed at Risk*, and *The Journal of Research and Development in Education*.

Acknowledgments

This book exists only because there are outstanding teachers, administrators, and support staff who have defied the odds and created outstanding urban schools. We not only respect, acknowledge, and appreciate your impressive work but also appreciate your willingness to open your schools to us and allow us to learn from your work. We hope this book is an affirmation of your impressive accomplishments, as well as a source of motivation as you continue to strive for excellence.

We also acknowledge and appreciate the many individuals—including school administrators, graduate students, professors, and teachers—who have engaged with us in visiting and studying America's high-performing urban schools. Your time, energy, and insights have been priceless as we have sought to better understand teaching and learning in outstanding urban schools.

We must also acknowledge that the study of high-performing urban schools is not new. Our work builds upon a tradition of scholarship and inquiry started by heroic educators such as Ron Edmonds, Larry Lezotte, and Wilbur Brookover and extended through the work of others such as Doug Reeves, James Scheurich, Karin Chenoweth, Mike Schmoker, Kati Haycock, and Linda Skrla. These leaders constructed the foundation upon which this effort was built.

We especially acknowledge the strong support of San Diego State University. The former university president, Stephen Weber, and the former dean of the university's College of Education, Lionel "Skip" Meno, envisioned a national center that would identify, study, and promote excellence in urban schools. They secured initial funding support from the Qualcomm Corporation, and they creatively sought/provided other support that helped us start the National Center for Urban School Transformation (NCUST). As an expression of their commitment to urban K–12 education, the university has continued this strong support, even in difficult financial times. The advocacy and support of the current university president, Elliot Hirshman, and the current dean of the College of Education, Ric Hovda, have helped NCUST thrive and grow

Finally, we acknowledge the time, wisdom, and commitment of our colleagues and staff at San Diego State University and at NCUST. We are honored to work with and learn from individuals who have committed themselves to supporting America's urban schools.

Introduction

Someone might ask, "Whatever happened to the American dream? Isn't this supposed to be the country where any child, regardless of race, ethnicity, language background, or family income, can aspire to academic, social, and economic success? Isn't this supposed to be the country where parents can expect that their children will grow up and enjoy a better standard of living than they experienced? What happened to the idea that every American child could access a quality education: a gateway to his or her dreams?"

Data suggest a different reality. High school graduation rates, standardized test scores, college completion rates, and almost any other indicator of academic accomplishment make the United States look more like a caste system than a nation of opportunity. One need consider only five variables—race/ethnicity, language background, family income, gender, and zip code—to accurately determine how the overwhelming majority of children will fare in our educational systems. What happened to the American dream?

The dream still lives in a few hundred remarkable schools across the nation. It has been our honor to identify, celebrate, and study amazing schools that achieve outstanding results for every demographic group they serve. This book is about schools that face impressive challenges associated with urban life—including poverty, crime, the lack of social services, and big-city bureaucracies—yet meet these challenges with impressive resolve, strong leadership, and effective teaching. Specifically, this book covers the nature of teaching in these schools. Through this book, we attempt to capture and describe the teaching practices that help set these high-performing schools apart from their more typical counterparts.

We hope that the information presented here can inspire, inform, and reinforce efforts to improve teaching and learning in thousands of urban schools in the United States. At the same time, we know that many practices described here are effectively implemented in schools that serve diverse populations of students in suburban and rural areas.

Our studies of outstanding schools have helped us understand that educators, through their daily practice in classrooms, can rekindle the American dream. Through this book, we endeavor to pass the flame.

1

Understanding and Using This Book

The National Center for Urban School Transformation (NCUST) is a research/service unit affiliated with the College of Education and the Department of Educational Leadership at San Diego State University. NCUST was established in 2005 with the help of an endowment from Qualcomm, Inc. In pursuit of its mission to support school districts in transforming urban schools, the center immediately began a program of identifying, celebrating, and studying elementary, middle, and high schools that were among the highest performing urban schools in the nation. The center published and disseminated a set of award criteria; solicited nominations from state superintendents, local urban superintendents, and award-winning schools; and began a rigorous process of identifying schools for the center's National Excellence in Urban Education Award.

The Schools We Studied

In this book, we present teaching practices in schools that won the National Excellence in Urban Education Award. The award criteria and the selection process (more fully described in Appendix A) required schools to demonstrate strong achievement results for every demographic group they served. Based on state standardized assessments, schools had to show evidence of strong academic accomplishment for every racial/ethnic group of students they served. In fact, schools had to demonstrate achievement levels for each racial/ethnic group that exceeded the average achievement rates for all students in the state. NCUST also expected strong indicators of academic success for English learners and students with disabilities. NCUST looked carefully at attendance rates, graduation rates, participation in advanced courses of study, suspension/expulsion rates, and a variety of other success indicators. The applicants included many National Blue Ribbon Schools, National Title I Distinguished Schools, schools recognized on *U.S. News & World Report*'s List of Best High Schools in America, and schools that earned a wide array of statewide distinctions. We selected as finalists the schools that presented the strongest evidence of academic success with all demographic groups of students.

We conducted on-site visits to every finalist school. Teams of researchers, teachers, and administrators (including educators from previous winning schools) visited finalist schools and spent considerable amounts of time observing classrooms; interviewing teachers, administrators, students, and parents; and reviewing student work. We observed teacher planning meetings, parent meetings, and staff meetings. We talked with district administrators and neighborhood leaders. But mostly, we spent time in classrooms.

Between 2006 and 2012, we awarded sixty-two schools from seventeen states (see Appendix B, page 135, for the full list of award winners). The schools included elementary, middle, and high schools of varying sizes and demographic compositions. Most of the award-winning schools are typical public schools that serve their surrounding neighborhoods. Some are in districts with open enrollment policies that allow students to attend any district school. Some are magnet or choice schools that attempt to attract students through a theme or curricular specialty. Some are public charter schools. Among these last two categories, NCUST only considered schools that accepted all students who sought admission or that admitted students based upon lotteries or first-come, first-served policies. Although we acknowledge that there are many outstanding public schools with selective admissions policies and many impressive private schools, we chose not to focus upon those schools. We focused upon schools that enroll typical urban students and attain very atypical results. This book is based upon our findings from these schools, especially the schools awarded from 2008 through 2012.

So, this book is not about our theories or philosophies; it is about the actual practices we found in schools that achieve outstanding academic results. This book is not about what we prescribe as means to generate strong results as much as it is about what we observed when we visited many of America's best urban schools.

It is also important to note that this book was influenced by our previous research and scholarship at Ohio State University and the University of Texas at Austin. Findings from our more current studies underscore the importance of the lessons we learned from high-performing schools during the 1990s and the early 2000s.

Focus on Teaching Practices

Many factors contributed to the success of these urban schools; however, a central factor was the nature and quality of teaching. Teaching in these high-performing schools was qualitatively different from teaching in urban schools that achieved mediocre academic results. Through this book, we explain how teaching was different in these high-performing urban schools. We relate how teaching looked, sounded, and felt. We dissect excellent, effective instruction in ways that make it more understandable and replicable.

We have been inspired by the effectiveness of instruction in high-performing urban schools. Students learned more because they were taught in ways that made it easier for them to learn. Students learned more because teachers worked systematically to ensure each student's progress. Ultimately, students learned more because teachers demanded nothing less of their students and of themselves.

Currently, many elementary and secondary school educators are concerned about the adoption of Common Core State Standards (CCSS). These new learning expectations are likely to demand the teaching of concepts and skills that are more rigorous than most existing state standards. It is exciting to note that in many of the schools featured in this book, we observed classrooms where students were demonstrating the academic knowledge and intellectual skills these new standards require. While many of the educators we studied would acknowledge that they have considerable work ahead as they aim to implement the standards fully, their teaching practices promote the depth of understanding and the applied use of knowledge that characterize the standards. We believe that to ensure all urban students master the standards, these teaching practices are essential.

Through our examination of many pages of field notes, observation records, and interviews of teachers, principals, and students, we condensed our findings into eight practices described in this book. As we shared our findings with leaders from several of these schools, they affirmed that these are the essential practices they envisioned and pursued.

We saw examples of the practices described in this book consistently but not universally throughout these schools. We never heard anyone at any of these high-performing schools claim perfection. In fact, principals, teachers, support staff, parents, and students were often impressively open in describing the areas where they still had room to grow. Nonetheless, in these high-performing urban schools, we found a significant core of teachers who regularly exhibited many of the practices described in this book.

Conversely, in our work with struggling schools, we often find a small number of teachers modeling the teaching practices we discuss in this book. Unfortunately, in struggling schools, best teaching practices seem to be best kept secrets because there is little effort to learn about and emulate these practices throughout the school.

It is important to note that we saw the same core practices in successful elementary, middle, and high schools. Certainly, high school math classes looked different from middle school social studies classes and even more different from primary-grade reading classes; however, the same core teaching practices were evident in classrooms across age groupings. The similarities in instructional practices were far more striking than the differences.

How to Use This Book

We believe that this book can have the greatest impact when teams of educators read, study, and use this book together. We hope that teachers, instructional coaches, department chairs, and school administrators come together to read and discuss the practices described in this book. Certainly, we believe that the practices described can be useful in urban elementary, middle, and high schools; however, we believe that the practices can help any school improve its effectiveness in ensuring that all children experience academic success. We hope that teams of educators come together and ask themselves, "How are our practices similar to and different from the practices described in this book?" In particular, we hope that educators will go into each other's classrooms so that they acquire objective information that helps them affirm their pedagogical strengths and identify opportunities for growth. While individuals can certainly use this book to hone their teaching practices, we have learned that teamwork is an essential ingredient in the success of outstanding schools. As well, we hope that this book is more than just a topic for the next random act of professional development. Instead, we hope that this book inspires a deep commitment to ongoing efforts to improve professional practice. As we note in Chapter 10, change requires focused, persistent effort. In order to change practices, teachers need many opportunities to try the practice, receive constructive feedback, reflect, refine, and try again.

How the Book Is Organized

Chapters 2 through 9 describe in detail each of the common instructional practices we found in these award-winning schools. Each chapter provides examples from lessons observed in actual classrooms within high-performing elementary, middle, and high schools. Also, as we describe each practice, we contrast it with practices we have seen in more typical urban schools. We try to explain in detail with rich examples and counter-examples.

Chapter 2 describes the focus on mastery that typified instruction in these schools. Teachers focused persistently and doggedly on leading all children to master explicit academic objectives. While many urban schools sabotage their improvement efforts by rigidly trying to "cover" all of the standards or by insisting that they "keep pace" with a pacing guide, these more successful schools chose to focus on getting their students to master key academic content (sometimes at the expense of ignoring some standards). This practice highlights the overarching sense of purpose that influences how the other seven practices are pursued.

Chapters 3 through 7 describe pedagogical techniques intended to maximize student understanding. Chapter 3 describes the manner in which teachers introduced new instructional content, while Chapter 4 describes how teachers sought to acquire evidence that each student understood the content being taught and how teachers responded to the evidence they acquired. Chapter 5 specifically focuses on the manner in which teachers designed lessons that were likely to build upon the backgrounds, cultures, and prior knowledge of students. Chapter 6 explains how teachers endeavored to ensure that students mastered the essential vocabulary associated with the lesson, and Chapter 7 explains how teachers promoted successful independent practice and minimized the time students spent "practicing" incorrectly.

The next two chapters focus largely on affective or relational practices. Chapter 8 describes the ways in which teachers in these high-performing schools made students feel valued, respected, and appreciated. Chapter 9 explains how teachers made students eager to learn more. One should not assume that these practices are less important than the ones described in the preceding six chapters. In fact, it is difficult to imagine these schools achieving success without a substantial mix of both the cognitive and the affective practices described here.

Each chapter (from Chapter 2 through 9) includes discussion of the practice and examples from the schools we visited and studied. Additionally, each chapter includes annotated suggested readings that describe research and best practices related to the practices described in the chapter. These suggested readings offer individuals or school teams opportunities to delve deeper into each practice, understand nuances, and better establish a clear vision of the teaching practices they want to develop.

Finally, each chapter (from Chapter 2 through 9) includes a practice guide that might be used in multiple ways. Teachers can use these guides as self-assessments. Teachers might ask themselves, "In my lesson today, how many of these items did I accomplish?" Alternately, among a group of teachers endeavoring to maximize a practice, teachers might use one of the guides to observe each other and provide feedback. Similarly, in schools committed to increasing a practice, administrators might use the guide as an organizing framework for professional development activities, as a tool for conducting classroom visits and observations, and/or as a vehicle for offering teachers feedback about the extent to which they are making progress in implementing the practice.

Each guide offers suggestions about evidence that might be indicative of the practice. As school teams consider the various guides, additional ideas may emerge as appropriate supplements or replacements. Each item is only a piece of evidence that may or may not reflect full implementation of the practice. Nonetheless, the guide may be helpful as educators seek to improve their implementation.

Even in outstanding lessons, it is rare to find "yes" answers to all of the items in a guide. A lesson is probably strong if half of the items are identified affirmatively. Great lessons might evidence three-fourths or more of the items.

In Chapter 10, the final chapter, we describe some factors that might inhibit educators from implementing these practices throughout their schools. At the same time, we highlight how some of the high-performing schools we studied overcame those barriers. How did leaders promote changes in practice? How did they inspire a willingness to change? How did they create consistency in the adoption of key practices across grade levels, departments, new teachers, and veterans?

Clearly, we must learn more about how schools developed these practices. How did they identify the practices that were most successful for educating their students? How did they help each other learn about and practice new teaching behaviors? How did they build the knowledge, skills, and commitment necessary to achieve these changes in pedagogy? How did they build the schedules, routines, and structures that supported their improvement efforts? How did they avoid implementation fatigue and sustain practices across time? In addition, we hope to learn more about the degree to which each of these practices influences achievement results. Are some practices more important? Are some starting points more likely to influence long-term success? This is only a beginning effort to describe what has rarely been described: the nature of instruction in high-achieving urban schools.

2

Focusing on Mastery

A science teacher at Horace Mann Dual Language Academy in Wichita, Kansas, explained (in Spanish) to her class of fifth-grade students that during the class period they would learn five concepts related to volcanic activity. She explained that by the end of the period, they would be able to describe (in Spanish) each of the five concepts and explain how the concepts were related. Immediately, she asked several students to describe (in Spanish) what they were going to learn during the lesson. Next, using Spanish vocabulary the students had previously mastered, the teacher explained each concept. Immediately after each explanation, she asked several students to explain the concept in their own words (in Spanish). After several students had explained each concept and students seemed fairly comfortable with the new vocabulary, the teacher invited pairs of students to come to the front of the room and pantomime a concept. Other students were expected to guess which concept the students were modeling. Every student was paying attention to the pantomimes, trying to be one of the first to guess the intended meaning. As students became more comfortable using the new vocabulary, the teacher asked additional questions that required students to explain the relationships among the concepts. The teacher asked questions of every student. If a student did not know the answer, the teacher asked another student, but within a few minutes returned to the initial student with the same question. In this way, each student felt responsible for paying attention and learning the content, even if they could not respond to the teacher's initial question. By the end of the lesson, students were using the new Spanish vocabulary comfortably. Students asked questions about important details. The teacher used those questions to deepen the conversation and teach more about volcanic activity. At the end of the period, as students left the classroom, the researcher stopped a few students and asked them what they had learned in class. In English, they explained the concepts they had learned, accurately and with impressive detail.

> *Horace Mann Dual Language Academy is in the Wichita Public School District in Wichita, Kansas. The school serves approximately 530 students in grades kindergarten through eight. The school won the National Excellence in Urban Education Award in 2009.*

■

Many U.S. teachers perceive that their job is to prepare and present a series of academic lessons, covering specific topics and specific academic standards, across an academic year. Of course, they are expected to fulfill this responsibility while simultaneously managing classroom and school routines, student behavior, paperwork, and other assorted duties; however, school districts and teacher-training institutions have led teachers to perceive that their job is primarily to organize and present academic content.

In contrast, we found a profound, albeit subtle, difference in the way teachers in high-performing urban schools perceived their work. These teachers acted as if their job was to ensure that their students mastered specific academic content and skills. For these teachers, presenting or covering content was not the goal. Instead, they focused upon leading students—all of their students—to demonstrate mastery of specific academic objectives. They persistently, and sometimes relentlessly, pursued student mastery. Teachers approached each lesson with a sense of mission. The mission was not to follow the teacher's guide, cover the chapter, or even present the relevant content. Instead, the mission was to help every student achieve a deep level of understanding and/or skill related to a specific academic concept.

Planning for Mastery

Like most teachers, teachers in the schools we studied planned. However, their planning was not focused simply on complying with a principal's mandate for a plan. They were not planning merely to ensure compliance with a district pacing chart. Instead, we found teachers who planned strategically how they would lead the specific students in their classrooms to master specific concepts and skills. The goal of planning was not coverage. Instead, the goal was student mastery.

For example, the science teacher at Horace Mann Dual Language Academy (described in the chapter opening) planned to ensure that her students would exit her classroom with a working knowledge of the five concepts she planned to teach that day. She was not content simply to cover pages in a textbook, provide a lecture, or show a video clip. She wanted to be sure that her students would understand each of the key concepts she wanted them to learn. She wanted to be sure that all of her students could discuss the concepts accurately, with some depth of understanding. She wanted to know that each and every student could distinguish among the concepts, describe, explain, compare, and contrast. Her goal was mastery, not coverage.

Because the goal of planning was student mastery, teachers planned with their students in mind. Teachers considered, "What do my students need to see, do, hear, touch, and experience in order to master this important concept?" Teachers considered the prior knowledge, backgrounds, and interests of their students. They considered the vocabulary students might have previously mastered and the vocabulary students were less likely to know well. They considered how textbooks and workbooks might help them guide their students toward mastery, but they also considered where published materials might fall short and other teaching aids, metaphors, manipulatives, technology, or experiences might help their students achieve mastery of the important academic concepts and skills they sought to teach.

Wiggins and McTighe (2005) encourage educators to focus less on "covering" content and more on planning lessons that lead students to master important content. In the award-winning schools we studied, we consistently found lessons that were planned to lead students to mastery.

Objective-Driven Lessons

Often, in our visits to high-performing schools, we heard teachers make statements such as, "Before this period ends, you will be able to explain why . . ." or "In today's class, you're going to show me that you know how to . . ." or "Before the bell rings, I expect each one of you to be able to describe the relationship between . . ." or "By 9:15, I want everyone to be able to describe in writing the steps for solving this kind of problem and explain why each step makes sense." Teachers in high-performing urban schools are explicit about what they want their students to learn. Typically, they write and post the specific learning objective that is the focus of instruction. But even more importantly, they talk about the learning objective with students. They help students know specifically, clearly, and explicitly what they should be attempting to learn. For example, throughout MacArthur High School in the Aldine Independent School District (Houston, Texas), teachers post a three-part objective that explains to students (1) what they are going to learn in the lesson, (2) how they are going to learn it, and (3) how they will know they have learned it. At National City Middle School in National City, California, teachers post the learning target for the day and ask students to focus upon the verb. "What are you going to do today?" an English teacher asked, prompting the students to respond, "Analyze." "And, what will you be analyzing?" he continued. "Character personality traits," a student answered before the teacher led students in a discussion of the specific meaning of this objective.

This is starkly different from classrooms in which teachers post "Math—pages 145–147" or "photosynthesis" as an "objective." In such classrooms, teachers let students know about the activity in which they will engage or the topic area they will address; however, students do not necessarily understand specifically what their teacher expects them to learn or understand.

These objective-driven lessons are also different from lessons in which teachers specify only a broad standard or learning goal. In some cases, a standard or a learning goal might encompass multiple objectives requiring a sequence of several lessons. For example, a broad standard might require students to understand fractional concepts. This standard could include a vast array of specific objectives, such as identifying fractional parts of a whole, converting improper fractions, and identifying equivalent fractions. Stating the standard or the learning goal might be helpful in giving students a picture of what they should ultimately learn; however, it might not help students understand what they should know or be able to do at the end of the day's lesson. In the highest performing schools, teachers recognize that they often need to identify and teach several objectives in order for their students to master a specific standard or learning goal. Teachers are explicit in defining the objective they want their students to learn at the moment, en route to mastery of challenging standards.

Frequently, in our visits to classrooms, we ask students what they are learning at that particular moment. In many typical urban schools, we hear students respond, "We're reading this story" or "I've got to finish this worksheet" or "I'm supposed to answer these questions." Their answers suggest that their goal is to complete the activity, do the assignment, or follow the routine. In contrast, in high-performing urban schools, students are much more likely to respond that they are learning a specific academic objective: "We're learning how to calculate the volume of a triangular prism" or "We're trying to determine the author's purpose in different kinds of texts" or "We're learning how heat influences the water cycle." In these classes, students know the lesson objective, often because it is posted and discussed. Teachers engage students in discussions concerning both what they will learn and why it is important.

It is important to note that in high-performing urban schools, objectives drive lessons. The activities implemented, the questions asked, the examples provided, the materials chosen, and the tasks assigned are heavily influenced by the objective. "Everything I do, from start to finish, is designed to teach my kids the particular objective I need them to learn," a teacher at Benjamin Franklin Elementary in Bakersfield, California, explained. Similarly, the principal of Thomas Henderson Middle School in Richmond, Virginia, insisted, "All of our instructional decisions are purposeful. We don't do things just because the textbook says or because that's the way we taught it last year. We do things to ensure students learn the objective."

In objective-driven lessons, teachers are constantly focused on what they want students to learn and how they want students to demonstrate they have learned it. While teachers attend to the objective, they also focus on how each student is progressing toward learning the objective. Teachers plan, monitor, and adjust their teaching so that there is a high likelihood that all students will master the lesson objective.

Depth of Understanding

A focus on mastery implies more than the pursuit of surface-level knowledge. In high-performing urban schools, many lessons are designed to generate a depth of understanding. Students are expected to analyze, explain, discuss, and apply in ways that exhibit mastery of the content. In these schools, superficial recall of facts is insufficient. For example, while many elementary school students may be expected to learn general facts about slavery and the Civil War, students in a social studies class at Charles Lunsford Elementary in Rochester, New York, were expected to assume the role of Abraham Lincoln's speechwriter. They worked in groups to write speeches that offered arguments against slavery, building from Lincoln's personal experiences. These students acquired a much greater understanding of both the personal history of Lincoln and the impact of slavery on human lives.

Arguably, teaching toward a depth of understanding may take more time than pursuing recall of general facts. Teachers in some schools may perceive that they do not have sufficient time to pursue depth. In high-performing urban schools, we found it common for principals to encourage teachers to pursue depth, even if it meant covering fewer topics (less breadth). Also, teachers in some of these schools reported that their students were less likely to forget concepts and skills when they took the time to pursue a depth of understanding. As a result, teachers could spend less time repeating and reviewing.

In mathematics instruction in high-performing urban schools, we found depth reflected in teaching that required students to answer "Why?" For example, students were not simply asked to "solve for X." They were also asked to explain why each step made sense. They were asked to explain what *solving for X* meant. They were asked to explain why their errors did not make sense. They were asked to apply their knowledge to real situations.

In high-performing urban schools, lesson objectives often specified the depth of knowledge the teacher wanted the students to acquire. For example, objectives might have specified that students would describe, explain, model, demonstrate, debate, justify, construct, or analyze. Accordingly, lessons were organized and presented in ways that were clearly intended to ensure that students would be able to demonstrate the depth of knowledge expected. So, if the objective suggested that students would model a concept, lesson activities were structured in a way that required students to model—and allowed the teacher to determine if students could, in fact, model—the concept. Teachers did not merely present information and hope that students would attain the desired depth of knowledge.

Time on Objective

As teachers in high-performing urban schools strive to help students master challenging academic content, they act as if every available minute is a precious resource. They rarely stray from the central concept or skill they are attempting to teach. They might approach the concept in different ways, use different examples, or teach different algorithms; however, they remain focused on the main concept or skill they want students to master.

Within high-performing urban schools, educators have worked together to find ways to minimize distractions. Intercom announcements, bells, and phone distractions have been curtailed or eliminated. Few, if any, students are pulled out of classrooms because special instructional personnel more typically work alongside the classroom teacher, within the regular classroom setting. Teachers and leaders have worked to minimize transition times and eliminate the time students spend waiting for instruction to commence. Routines are finely tuned so that the maximum amount of time possible can be devoted to learning.

In some more typical schools, educators might focus upon maximizing time on task: the time students spend working on an assigned task. In contrast, in high-performing urban schools, teachers are more focused on maximizing the amount of time students spend learning specific academic objectives. We saw few "filler" activities and almost no busywork. We did not observe students spending large amounts of time copying information, coloring, or completing tasks that required minimal thinking. Often, lesson objectives required students to engage in higher-level thinking processes such as describing, analyzing, comparing, explaining, or evaluating, so lesson activities frequently engaged students in dialogue that encouraged these mental activities. Of course, there were times when students copied information or colored pictures; however, in high-performing urban schools, those types of activities consumed a much smaller percentage of time compared to the percentage of time they consume in typical urban schools.

In high-performing urban schools, lessons rarely end before the class period ends. Teachers eagerly use minutes at the end of the period to check to ensure that students have mastered the objective taught. From start to finish, each lesson fills the available time, not simply because teachers are complying with administrative demands but also because teachers want to ensure that true mastery has occurred.

Focusing on All Students

Teachers in these high-performing schools were not content to see a few or several students master the content they attempted to teach. They insisted upon high levels of engagement from all students because they wanted every student to exhibit mastery. At Marble Hill High School for International Studies in the Bronx, New York, teachers asserted that they never gave up on a student. One teacher explained, "In our school, we just don't give up . . . as long as a problem continues, we will continue to address it."

In more typical urban schools, we found classrooms where teachers seemed satisfied if students looked as if they were paying attention. In some classrooms, teachers seemed to be pleased if students were simply not being disruptive. In some classrooms of twenty, twenty-five, thirty, or more students, teachers provided a monologue or engaged in dialogue with only one or two students, while other students sat quietly, some with vacant expressions, some with their heads on their desks, some reading material completely unrelated to the lesson, and even some sleeping.

In contrast, in high-performing urban schools, teachers refused to allow students to sit passively and fail to learn. Teachers insisted that all students participate, engage, think, discuss, contribute, and make academic progress. Much of the substance of the following seven chapters explains how teachers created classroom environments in which student engagement was likely. In other words, teachers employed a variety of cognitive and affective practices that maximized the likelihood of active student participation.

While examining the subsequent chapters, keep in mind that teachers in these high-performing schools were particularly eager to ensure the engagement of groups of students who traditionally have not achieved well. For example, teachers were particularly deliberate in ensuring the engagement of English learners, students with disabilities, highly mobile students, students with lower reading abilities, and students who had histories of discipline problems. In fact, students from these groups often made substantial, and sometimes dramatic, academic gains because their teachers made persistent, conscientious, multipronged efforts to generate this high level of engagement among students who often become invisible in more typical urban schools.

In almost all of the high-performing urban schools we visited, students with mild or moderate disabilities received special services primarily in their regular classrooms. For example, at Louisa May Alcott in Cleveland, Ohio, special education personnel worked alongside general classroom teachers to help ensure that students with disabilities achieved the same academic results expected for all students. Special educators assumed responsibility for helping ensure that students with disabilities mastered the objectives that other students were being taught. Even when these students did not master the objective, they showed evidence of important academic gains that placed them closer to grade-level expectations. Special education was made "special" by the intensity of the effort to get students to master the general education curriculum. Specialists worked in collaboration with general education teachers to plan and implement a quality of services that led many students with disabilities to achieve grade-level proficiency.

In some schools, like Stephens Elementary in Houston, Texas (Aldine Independent School District), many English learners were served in separate bilingual classes; however, we consistently observed the teachers in the bilingual classes pursuing the same academic objectives with the same level of rigor as observed in classrooms taught exclusively in English. Bilingual education was not a separate track with different academic goals. Instead, bilingual classes offered a parallel route to the same high academic expectations held for all students throughout the school.

Similarly, at Nathan Adams Elementary in Dallas, Texas, native Spanish-speaking students and native English-speaking students learned the same content, read the same books, and did the same work at the same high levels of achievement, regardless of the language of instruction. The language of instruction is a tool for ensuring that all students achieve high levels of academic success.

This pursuit of mastery for all students might be considered an overarching theme to describe teaching in high-performing urban schools. The other practices discussed in this book all contribute to the effort to generate high levels of engagement and mastery among all students. Specifically, the mastery-oriented practiced we observed included efforts to present lessons in a logical, clear, and concise manner (Chapter 3); acquire and respond to evidence of understanding (Chapter 4); connect lesson objectives with students' interests, backgrounds, cultures, and prior knowledge (Chapter 5); make the lesson vocabulary part of students' conversational vocabulary (Chapter 6); promote practice opportunities that were likely to build and reinforce academic success (Chapter 7); interact with students in ways that made them feel valued, respected, and appreciated (Chapter 8); and provide lessons that were interesting and stimulating so that students were likely to learn to love learning (Chapter 9).

Ultimately, the focus on mastery is more than a teaching practice. It is the attitude, the orientation, the sense of urgency, the reason for teaching we noticed as we entered classrooms and observed teachers and students interact. Perhaps the best way of describing this focus was offered several years before we began our current study. In 1998, the principal of Brazosport High School in Brazosport, Texas, was interviewed in a study of high-performing schools. Achievement results had improved dramatically and earned the school an exemplary rating in the state's accountability system. The principal, Mr. Boone, was asked to describe the primary differences between his school then and his school several years prior, when the school's academic results had been dismal. After pondering a few moments, the principal replied, "Well, back then [prior to the school's improvement], we taught school like we were feeding the chickens." When the interviewer asked for clarification, the principal gave the following explanation:

> When you feed the chickens, you strap on your bag of feed and go out into the yard and toss the feed onto the ground. If the chickens eat the feed, that's fine. If they don't, that's fine. Your job is just to toss it out there. That's the way we taught school. We strapped on our lesson plans, we went into our classrooms, and we tossed out the information. If the students got it, fine. If the students didn't get it, fine. Back then, we thought our job was just to present the information, to toss it out there. The difference now is that our teachers want to see evidence that students have taken it in, ingested it, and digested the information. We don't stop until we see evidence that students have understood what we want them to learn. That's the main difference between our school back then and our school today.

Similarly, one might say that this is the main difference between schools with a focus on mastery and other schools. In the sixty-two high-performing schools we awarded and studied, consistently we saw teachers who were not satisfied to present the material, follow the lesson plan, pass out the worksheets, or otherwise "toss the feed." Instead, they were determined to ensure that students learned, absorbed, understood, and applied the specific objective of their lesson.

What It Is & What It Isn't
Focusing on Mastery

■ *What It Is*

Focusing on getting students to understand specific content or skills

Example: The objective posted on the board reads, "Students will make and justify logical inferences based upon nonfiction, grade-level text." At the beginning of the lesson, the teacher discusses the objective with the students and helps them understand what they should be able to do by the lesson's end. At various points during the lesson, the teacher reminds students that they are becoming more skillful at making and justifying logical inferences. Throughout the lesson, the teacher asks questions and poses tasks designed to get students to demonstrate their understanding of the concept of inference. As well, the teacher's questions help her understand how well students make and justify inferences based upon the nonfiction, grade-level text they are using.

What It Isn't

Focusing on "covering" a set of concepts, skills, or pages during the period/ day/unit

Example: The objective posted on the board reads, "Inferences." While the teacher covers information about inferences from the teacher's manual, she never explains the objective to students. She covers the material without ascertaining if students have any understanding of the concept or any ability to make and justify logical inferences.

■ What It Is

Planning with a focus on increasing the likelihood students will understand the specific concept/skill by the end of the lesson

Example: The teacher plans three or four different activities that are likely to help her students understand the concept she wants them to learn. The teacher anticipates what students will need to know in order to make sense of the concept. The teacher plans questions she might pose or tasks she might design that would help her determine if students are progressing appropriately toward mastery. Also, in planning, the teacher anticipates possible inaccurate answers and possible misconceptions. She deliberately plans activities, examples, and illustrations that will help avoid misconceptions and maximize the likelihood that all students will achieve mastery.

What It Isn't

Planning with a focus on covering the pages in the text, following the manual, or completing available worksheet pages

Example: The teacher plans by following the outline of the teacher's manual and adds a few worksheets that are somewhat related to the objective.

■ What It Is

Constantly monitoring and assessing to determine if students are making sense of the lesson content and adapting instruction accordingly

Example: The geometry teacher planned a lesson to teach students how to find the volume of spheres, cylinders, and cones. As the teacher listens to student responses, she realizes that some students are confusing strategies for finding the volume of these solid objects with strategies for finding the volume of various polygonal prisms. She modifies the lesson by creating a T-chart on the front board. On the left side of the T-chart, she draws pictures of different polygonal prisms and asks students to describe the strategy for finding the volume of each. Then, on the right side, she draws examples of spheres, cylinders, and cones. When she asks students how to find the volume of these solid shapes, students begin to see that they were applying the same strategies they used for polygonal prisms. "Why would the formula for finding the volume of a cylinder be different from the formula for finding the volume of a rectangular prism?" she asks. Students explain that the size of a round base is likely to be different than the size of a rectangular base. Now the distinctions make sense.

What It Isn't

Focusing on covering the lesson precisely as it was planned

Example: The geometry teacher planned a lesson to teach students how to find the volume of spheres, cylinders, and cones. The teacher motors through the lesson as planned, even though some students seem to confuse strategies for finding the volume of these solid objects with strategies for finding the volume of polygonal prisms.

■ What It Is

Aiming to get students to demonstrate a thorough understanding of a concept or skill

Example: The teacher focuses upon getting students to explain *why* an algorithm centered upon identifying least common denominators and equivalent fractions works when they add fractions with unlike denominators.

What It Isn't

Aiming to get students to demonstrate a surface-level understanding

Example: The teacher focuses upon getting students to solve problems involving the addition of fractions with unlike denominators.

■ What It Is

Working to keep students engaged in efforts to better understand the lessons objective

Example: The teacher engages students in four different learning centers. Three of the centers provide opportunities for students to practice the objective she is teaching/reinforcing through guided instruction to small groups. A fourth center provides opportunities for students to practice a recently mastered objective. When the lesson ends, students are more likely to have achieved mastery of the lesson's primary objective because three of the four centers gave students opportunities to practice various aspects of the objective.

What It Isn't

Working to keep students busy throughout the class period

Example: The teacher engages students in four different learning centers, each focused on a different objective, while she provides guided instruction to a small group on another objective.

■ *What It Is*

Expecting each and every student to work toward mastery of challenging objectives, providing support to students who need special assistance, and providing enrichment opportunities that keep students feeling challenged

Example: The teacher plans lesson activities in consideration of her students' wide range of abilities. When she recognizes that some students are having difficulty completing the assignment independently, she provides intensive assistance designed to help them understand. On the other hand, she gives students who complete the assignment early a "may do" assignment that requires them to pursue the objective at a deeper level.

What It Isn't

Expecting students with specific learning needs to pursue different, lesser, and often unrelated learning objectives and expecting students who demonstrate success quickly to sit and wait

Example: The teacher plans one major lesson activity for all students. Students who have difficulty completing the assignment (because they do not understand the content) turn in blank papers. Students who complete the assignment early are expected to sit quietly.

■ *What It Is*

Refusing to allow students to sit passively and fail

Example: A teacher calls upon students randomly (whether they raise their hands or not). If students appear disengaged, the teacher is even more likely to ask them to respond, demonstrate, or somehow become engaged in the lesson.

What It Isn't

Allowing students to sit quietly and do little, as long as they do not disrupt the teacher or their classmates

Example: A teacher only calls upon students who want to be called upon. Other students are free to sit quietly, daydream, or occupy themselves quietly.

Practice Guide Related to Focusing on Mastery

For information on possible uses of this practice guide, please see pages 5–6 in Chapter 1.

1. Was the objective posted?   Y   N

2. Was the objective posted in language students were likely to understand?   Y   N

3. Did the posted objective match the objective being taught?   Y   N

4. Was the lesson objective influencing the teacher's actions throughout the lesson? (Did the objective—not the textbook, a worksheet, or a teacher's manual—drive the lesson?)   Y   N

5. If an observer asked students to describe the objective being taught, could each student offer an appropriate description?   Y   N

6. At various times throughout the lesson, did the teacher remind students of the objective being taught?   Y   N

7. Were all lesson activities/discussions focused on the lesson objective?   Y   N

8. Did lesson activities reflect careful planning intended to result in students' mastering the specific objective?   Y   N

9. Did the lesson require students to use higher cognitive skills than recall or memorization?   Y   N

10. Were the lesson activities designed to help students achieve the depth of knowledge articulated in the lesson objective?   Y   N

11. Did the lesson occur without significant distractions?   Y   N

12. Were transition times minimized?   Y   N

13. Were more than 90 percent of the students focused on the objective at least 90 percent of the time?   Y   N

14. Are at least 50 percent of the students likely to show mastery of the content taught during the lesson?   Y   N

15. Are at least 75 percent of the students likely to show mastery of   Ⓨ   Ⓝ
the content taught during the lesson?

16. Are at least 90 percent of the students likely to show mastery   Ⓨ   Ⓝ
of the content taught during the lesson?

In a strong lesson, a "yes" answer is recorded for at least eight of these items.
In an outstanding lesson, a "yes" answer is recorded for at least twelve of these items.

Suggested Readings Related to Focusing on Mastery

Mastery is not a new idea in education. The following articles and books describe research, scholarship, and best practices related to the major ideas presented in this chapter.

Blackburn, B. R. (2012). *Rigor made easy: Getting started.* Larchmont, NY: Eye On Education.

> A focus on mastery requires a commitment to depth of understanding versus coverage of material. Blackburn emphasizes this point in Chapter 2 of her book as she provides practical suggestions for increasing the level of rigor in classrooms.

Bloom, B. S. (1971). Mastery learning. In J. H. Block (Ed.), *Mastery learning: Theory and practice* (pp. 47–63). New York: Holt, Rinehart, & Winston.

> In this classic article, the author describes mastery learning as an antidote for traditional bell-curve notions of student aptitude and achievement and one-size-fits-all instruction. Bloom argues that we can get most students to master content if we teach in ways that address their learning needs.

Guskey, T. R. (2007, Fall). Closing achievement gaps: Revisiting Benjamin S. Bloom's "Learning for Mastery." *Journal of Advanced Academics*, pp. 8–31.

> In this article, Guskey describes the use of Bloom's mastery approach as a tool for closing achievement gaps. Guskey explains that the positive effects of mastery learning extend beyond cognitive or academic outcomes to improvements in students' confidence as learners, school attendance rates, and attitudes toward and engagement in learning.

Hattie, J. A. C. (2009). *Visible learning: A synthesis of over 800 meta-analyses relating to achievement.* Abingdon, Oxon: Routledge.

> This meta-analysis of research studies reports the extent to which various practices influence student achievement. In particular, the

author notes that teaching strategies that emphasize learning intentions (e.g., clear learning goals and behavior objectives) have high effect sizes. In Chapter 11, the author synthesizes these studies in a way that reflects the importance of the teacher's focus on student mastery.

Marzano, R. J. (2007). *The art and science of teaching: A comprehensive framework for effective instruction.* Alexandria, VA: Association for Supervision and Curriculum Development.

Chapter 1 of Marzano's book describes the research that underscores the importance of a focus on specific learning goals, rubrics, and feedback aligned to the learning goals. The chapter offers practical examples that might be useful to educators.

McKenzie, K. B., & Skrla, L. (2011). *Using equity audits in the classroom to reach and teach all students.* Thousand Oaks, CA: Corwin.

This book offers practical suggestions for exploring issues of equity and excellence in schools. While the book offers many helpful ideas, the concept of active cognitive engagement (ACE) might be particularly helpful as educators consider how they focus on mastery for each student.

Nuthall, G. (2005). The cultural myths and realities of teaching and learning: A personal journey. *Teachers College Record, 107*(5), 895–934.

After forty-five years of research on teaching and learning in classrooms, Nuthall concluded that teachers typically do not focus on mastery. Instead, they focus more on keeping students busy and carrying out routines. The author suggests that a more productive approach would be to shape instructional practices in ways that are more likely to promote student mastery.

Saphier, J., Haley-Speca, M. A., & Gower, R. (2008). *The skillful teacher: Building your teaching skills.* Acton, MA: Research for Better Teaching.

A focus on mastery begins with a teacher's beliefs about her students' capacity to learn and her capacity to teach. Chapter 2 of this book explores the importance of these beliefs and their impact on teaching.

Wiggins, G. P., & McTighe, J. (2005). *Understanding by design* (Expanded 2nd ed.). Upper Saddle River, NJ: Pearson Education, Inc.

This book emphasizes an approach to teaching that is consistent with the focus on mastery described in this chapter. The authors emphasize, "The job of teaching is to optimize student learning of what is worthy—not to 'cover' a book, nor to 'teach, test and hope for the best,' irrespective of [learning] results" (p. 314).

3

Introducing Content Logically, Clearly, and Concisely

A fifth-grade teacher at Highland Elementary was teaching his students to understand linear equations. In a prior lesson, students had learned about variables. In this lesson, the focus was on mathematic expressions. The teacher succinctly explained to students that an algebraic expression combined a variable and a value. He provided a variety of practical examples and then engaged the students in brainstorming many additional examples.

One student offered, "Like the number of points your team gets for a score could be a variable and the number of scores could be the value."

"Yes," the teacher responded. "So, what might an expression be for three scores?"

"Three S," the student answered proudly.

"Exactly! So, what does the expression 'Three S' mean?" the teacher asked a different student.

"It means three times an unknown number," the student answered.

"An unknown number of what?" the teacher probed?

"An unknown number of scores," stated another child.

Students were then directed to list expressions on sentence strips and then, on separate sentence strips, write out words that would indicate what the expressions meant. Later students played a matching game in which they matched the sentence strips by pairing the algebraic expressions with the matching word sentences.

Highland Elementary is in the Montgomery County Public School District in Silver Spring, Maryland. The school serves approximately 450 students in grades pre-kindergarten through five. The school won the National Excellence in Urban Education Award in 2009.

■

Mastery is not achieved by accident. The manner in which teachers introduce content accelerates or decelerates student understanding. Students master more when teachers introduce content logically, clearly, and concisely. In high-performing urban schools, teachers introduce information in ways that make it easier for students to understand. They plan instruction so that mastery is likely. This starts, as Chapter 3 implies, with clarity about what students are expected to learn. Effective teachers know specifically what they want to students to master, and they know what they will accept as evidence of mastery. Unlike teachers who might just "cover" the chapter, follow the teacher's guide, or read the script, effective teachers know what they want students to be able to explain, analyze, discuss, solve, perform, or otherwise demonstrate, and they know how well they want students to be able to perform. While these teachers start with the "end in mind," they plan instruction that students are likely to perceive as clear, logical, and understandable.

Logical Introduction of Content, One Step at a Time

In high-performing urban schools, formally or informally, teachers create and follow logical task analyses as the means to help children build strong understanding of various key concepts and skills. In the math lesson at Highland Elementary (described in the chapter opening), the teacher did not rush to present the entire concept of linear equations in one lesson. Instead, he carefully worked to help students build an understanding of all of the components. He carefully considered what students needed to understand at each rung of the ladder. Logically and systematically, he moved students from one key concept to the next.

In more typical lessons, often the ladder toward understanding is missing rungs. Textbooks and workbooks are often constructed to cover large amounts of material in a minimal number of pages. Sometimes concepts with three, four, or more important components are presented briefly with little or no attention to the important sequence of details that might bolster student understanding. If teachers rely heavily on such teaching tools, their students may experience confusion and frustration.

The task of dividing learning goals into logical steps may not be necessary when one is teaching simple concepts with minimal depth. In contrast, logical, sequential presentations may be essential as teachers focus upon Common Core State Standards and other learning goals that require substantial utilization of higher-order thinking skills. In high-performing urban schools, we observed teachers tackling rigorous, complex academic standards by identifying a logical sequence of specific objectives students needed to learn in order to master the standard.

Several researchers have referred to the process of breaking complex concepts and skills into logical steps as "chunking." Marzano (2007) briefly summarizes this research and explains the importance of organizing information into "digestible chunks for students" (p. 34).

Teachers are much better equipped to help students pursue mastery when teachers possess deep knowledge of the content they intend to teach. Teachers must be able to identify the subconcepts and subskills that will influence mastery. They must be able to predict the issues that might confuse and frustrate students if students do not understand them well. Through their own mastery of the content, teachers are better able to plan and deliver a logical sequence of lessons and a logical sequence of activities within a lesson, leading students to deeper levels of understanding.

High-performing urban schools do not simply acquire teachers with great content knowledge. They continuously work to build teachers' content knowledge through excellent teacher-to-teacher collaboration. By collaboratively planning how they will lead students to deep levels of mastery, teachers collectively build their own content mastery. By sharing and examining student work products, teachers learn from each other's insights, knowledge, and skills.

While many schools claim to promote teacher collaboration, sometimes the efforts fall short of influencing improvement in teaching and learning. In contrast, in the high-performing urban schools we studied, collaboration was keenly focused upon, helping teachers deepen their expertise. For example, at Nueva Vista Elementary School in Los Angeles, California, teachers worked together in professional learning communities that resulted in substantial improvements in the quality of instruction throughout the school. Similarly, at Escontrias Elementary in El Paso, Texas (Socorro Independent School District), teachers meet in grade-level teams and in vertical teams to discuss the content they intend to teach. In the vertical teams, teachers meet with teachers at other grade levels who share leadership responsibility for specific subject areas (e.g., mathematics or reading). Teachers engage in detailed conversation about what needs to be learned at each grade level in order to ensure that students are ready to succeed at the next grade level. In grade-level team meetings, teachers discuss what students will need to master in order to meet specific learning expectations. They discuss the intricacies of what students must master in ways that help build their own content knowledge. Also, the teachers will share and discuss student work and give particular attention to the nature of instruction that led some students to higher levels of mastery.

It is important to note that sometimes delivery of a more logical sequence of lessons takes more time than is often allotted in district pacing guides. As mentioned in Chapter 2, in high-performing urban schools, we found it common for principals to encourage teachers to pursue depth, even if it meant covering a few less topics. Fewer concepts may have been covered, but more concepts were mastered in depth, in part because teachers were careful to identify and deliberately teach the concepts and skills students needed to learn in order to attain mastery of challenging academic standards.

Clarity Is a Virtue

In high-performing urban schools, teachers present information in ways that are clear, direct, and easy to understand. Certainly, the logical sequencing of instruction helps make lessons clear. Additionally, however, we found that teachers in high-performing urban schools try to make sure that students understand the first concept before they proceed to teach the second.

In contrast, sometimes textbooks and worksheets push teachers to introduce multiple concepts and then immediately ask students to distinguish the ideas from each other. This sometimes results in the "stump the students" game in which teachers pose a question that students have little chance of answering correctly; often the only student who knows the answer is a child who had mastered the concepts long before the teacher introduced them. Sometimes, in these situations, students begin making wild guesses that consume time, without leading students to stronger fundamental understandings.

Generally, teachers in high-performing urban schools check meticulously to ensure that students understand one concept before they ask students to distinguish the concept from related concepts and ideas. Teachers work to ensure that students form clear mental images of one idea before they introduce another idea that could be a source of confusion.

Clarity is often enhanced through the use of graphic organizers and nonverbal representations. For example, we have observed teachers using pictures, charts, three-dimensional objects, graphs, concept maps, diagrams, and other tools to help students form a clear understanding of a concept or an idea. It is as if teachers have asked themselves the question, "What can I show my students that would make this concept clear to them?" Teachers understand that clarity may be difficult to achieve when they rely solely upon written or spoken language, especially when they are using language that is different from the language children typically hear outside of school.

Of course, in many cases, clarity is further enhanced as students are guided to create the pictures, charts, concept maps, and so forth on their own. These nonverbal representations can be particularly powerful when helping students grasp complex, abstract ideas with multiple components. For example, at Hambrick Middle School in Houston, Texas (Aldine Independent School District), we observed social studies students who used graphic organizers to clarify the differences between the Articles of Confederation and the U.S. Constitution. The graphic organizers helped students articulate key concepts so they were able to write detailed reports that made the distinctions clear to readers. Similarly, we observed fourth-grade students at Bridesburg Elementary in Philadelphia, Pennsylvania, select and use graphic organizers to help them develop expository papers concerning Vietnam.

Just as clarity is facilitated visually, it is also enhanced through auditory means. In high-performing schools, we observed teachers clearly and audibly articulating important ideas. They pronounced words accurately and distinctly, especially when those words were central to the concepts they were teaching. Teachers used vocabulary students understood, while causing students to recall and apply newly introduced vocabulary. Similarly, when teachers engaged students in responding orally (which occurred frequently, as described in Chapter 4), they insisted that students speak audibly and clearly so other students could learn from the conversation. Teachers often encouraged students to pronounce important vocabulary accurately and distinctly.

Clarity requires planning. Teachers reported that they spent considerable time planning (often with their colleagues) in ways that helped develop lessons students were likely to understand. Teachers planned in ways that considered not only the content to be learned but also the students who were being asked to learn the content. As teachers at Escontrias Elementary planned, they anticipated possible student thinking errors and designed lessons that had a higher likelihood of leading students to an accurate understanding of key concepts.

Frequently, planning in high-performing urban schools includes a focus on anticipating possible misconceptions or sources of confusion or examining student work to identify the thinking errors that may be prompting incorrect answers. Such rigorous planning allows teaching to increase the clarity of instruction and better ensure student success.

Ultimately, clarity is in the mind of the beholder. What is clear to the teacher may not be clear to the student. By asking students to restate key concepts and ideas, many teachers made certain that students clearly understood important concepts. Even when teachers had worked together to plan detailed, well-sequenced, clear lessons, they checked to make sure that students could use their own words to describe or explain the major concepts teachers wanted their students to learn. This practice of checking understanding is described in greater detail in Chapter 4.

Concise Presentations

Teachers in high-performing schools help students master new content by keeping presentations brief. Rarely did we observe long lectures. Overwhelmingly, we heard student voices more than we heard teacher voices as we visited classrooms. Often teachers would present a concept in a few minutes and immediately begin engaging students in discussion of the concept. By keeping the presentation of information brief, teachers forced themselves to be clear and concise. Students knew precisely what they were expected to learn and how they were expected to apply or use the new information.

In many cases, teachers were able to be more concise because they were teaching students strategies for accessing information and finding answers on their own. In other words, many teachers did not present all of the information they wanted students to learn and then hope students would remember all of the lecture's contents. Instead, teachers presented important core ideas and helped students learn how to access information quickly and reliably. For example, the aforementioned teacher of the social studies class at Charles Lunsford Elementary in Rochester, New York, did not offer a lengthy lecture concerning the various facets of life during the Civil War. Instead, she offered a clear explanation of the role she wanted her students to assume as speechwriters for Abraham Lincoln. She explained the importance of the task and she offered them a cart full of library books from which they could draw general ideas, specific facts, and compelling anecdotes.

By teaching students strategies for acquiring information, teachers can proceed more quickly to challenging academic tasks than they could if they tried to get students to memorize all of the information that is more typically perceived as prerequisite knowledge. For example, in several high-performing elementary schools, teachers reported that they were able to help students progress to more advanced mathematics, even though students had not memorized all of the multiplication facts. Teachers explained that they taught students strategies for getting the correct answer reliably and relatively quickly. A teacher at Signal Hill Elementary in Long Beach, California, explained, "We could get just about every student to learn to multiply by one, two, three, four, five, and ten. It was harder to get some students to master the rest of the facts. So, we started teaching students how to use the distributive property to make multiplication easy. If they wanted to multiply eight times six, we showed them that it's the same as multiplying eight times five and adding eight times one." This teacher taught her students a strategy that allowed them to acquire the correct answer reliably. Although students may not have initially demonstrated automaticity with multiplication facts, as many teachers desire, they acquired correct answers and developed a greater sense of personal efficacy concerning mathematics. By consistently acquiring the correct answer, students increased the likelihood of eventual memorization. In the meantime, students were able to advance to more complex mathematical concepts and skills.

Teachers were also able to spend less time presenting information when they helped students learn how to use rubrics or scoring guides to evaluate the quality of their work. Often teachers gave students rubrics before students began working. Sometimes, they engaged students in helping create the scoring rubric. Often, teachers in high-performing schools prompted students to use rubrics as students were completing assignments. This not only resulted in less teacher presentation time but also resulted in students' perceiving that they could ensure their academic success.

The logical, clear, and concise lessons we observed helped students acquire greater levels of mastery than we see in more typical urban schools.

Teachers worked diligently and collaboratively to plan, organize, and deliver instruction that made challenging concepts understandable.

What It Is &What It Isn't
Introducing Content Logically, Clearly, and Concisely

■ **What It Is**

Breaking down complex tasks into logical step-by-step sequences and teaching one step at a time

Example: The teacher wants students to be able to describe and discuss the factors that led the German people to follow Hitler, but first she devotes a lesson to helping students understand the sanctions imposed upon Germany at the end of World War I. Then she helps students understand the economic strife experienced by Germany and other nations during the 1930s.

What It Isn't

Teaching complex tasks without identifying, distinguishing, or sequencing the steps involved

Example: The teacher presents the chapter on the causes of World War II as one lesson with a huge mix of facts, dates, personalities, and contexts.

■ **What It Is**

Making sure students attain clarity regarding one concept before advancing to the next related concept

Example: The music teacher explains what quarter notes are, models examples of playing quarter notes, and gives students multiple opportunities to play quarter notes. When the teacher is fairly certain that students understand quarter notes, he introduces the concept of triplets.

What It Isn't

Trying to get students to differentiate related ideas before they have clarity about any of the ideas being taught

Example: The teacher plays quarter notes, then plays half notes, and then plays triplets. Immediately, the teacher asks students to distinguish between the three types of notes.

■ **What It Is**

Enhancing clarity through visual representations

Example: The teacher helps students create Venn diagrams that illustrate the similarities and differences of plant and animal cells. Then students use their diagrams as visual aids as they report their findings to peers.

What It Isn't

Expecting students to understand simply by reading text or listening to a lecture

Example: Students read the chapter about plant and animal cell characteristics and then answer the questions at the chapter's end.

■ *What It Is*

Checking to ensure that content, directions, and concepts are perceived clearly by all students

Example: The teacher asks students to write a letter to a friend that explains the steps the friend should use when he or she attempts to identify a pattern in a sequence of numbers. While students are writing, the teacher checks to ensure that students are explaining the steps accurately and clearly.

What It Isn't

Assuming that students perceive what is presented clearly

Example: The teacher lists the steps students should use when they attempt to identify a pattern in a sequence of numbers. Then the teacher asks, "Any questions?" When no students respond, the teacher tells students to begin. Then the teacher goes to his desk to grade homework papers.

■ *What It Is*

Anticipating possible misconceptions and teaching to prevent them

Example: As the elementary teachers plan how they will teach the concept of area of polygons, they recognize the possibility that students will confuse area with perimeter. They design a set of experiences that will first engage students in studying the etymology of the term *perimeter*; engage students in identifying, practicing, and discussing common uses of the term *area*; and then explore the difficulty of describing the size of a space without using square measurements. Finally, they engage students in choosing to use *perimeter tools* (rulers, yarn, yardsticks, and popsicle sticks) or *area tools* (one-centimeter square tiles, one-inch square tiles, and one-foot square tiles) to measure a variety of objects in the classroom. They plan to require students to articulate their rationale for their choice of measurement tools.

What It Isn't

Presenting without considering possible student misconceptions

Example: The teachers forge ahead into teaching the concept of area, without considering possible confusion with perimeter.

■ *What It Is*

Keeping presentations of information brief

Example: The teacher presents short two-minute clips from a movie. Each clip includes examples of characters using figurative language. After each clip, the teacher engages students in a discussion of the examples and types of figurative language observed.

What It Isn't

Long presentations

Example: The teacher presents a feature-length film with many great examples of characters using figurative language. At the conclusion of the film, the teacher asks students to recall some of the examples of figurative language used in the film.

■ *What It Is*

Teaching students strategies

Example: The teacher explains to students that they can identify an example of an author's use of personification through a two-step process. First, they identify where the author mentions a nonhuman object. Second, they look to determine if the author describes the nonhuman object in a way that would typically be used to describe a person.

What It Isn't

Expecting students to "figure it out"

Example: The teacher explains what personification means, highlights some examples of personification, and then asks students to identify and copy examples of personification found in a poem.

■ *What It Is*

Teaching students how to access information

Example: The teacher helps students identify key words they can use on a variety of search engines to access grade-appropriate information about the Lincoln-Douglas debates. Students then use the search engines to acquire information and organize a report of major themes and arguments from the debates.

What It Isn't

Expecting students to memorize information

Example: The teacher presents a lecture about the Lincoln-Douglas debates. Students are expected to take notes and remember major themes and arguments from the debates.

Practice Guide Related to Introducing Content Logically, Clearly, and Concisely

For information on possible uses of this practice guide, please see pages 5–6 in Chapter 1.

1. Did instruction reflect the teacher's mastery of the content being taught?　　　Ⓨ Ⓝ

2. Did the teacher break down complex ideas, concepts, or tasks into logical steps and teach one at a time?　　　Ⓨ Ⓝ

3. Did the teacher anticipate possible misunderstandings and teach accordingly?　　　Ⓨ Ⓝ

4. Did students understand/follow the presentation of information?　　　Ⓨ Ⓝ

5. Did the teacher ensure student mastery of one concept before presenting a second one?　　　Ⓨ Ⓝ

6. Could all students hear the instruction well?　　　Ⓨ Ⓝ

7. Did students restate important rules, procedures, or concepts?　　　Ⓨ Ⓝ

8. Did the teacher use nonverbal representations in order to make the information clearer to students?　　　Ⓨ Ⓝ

9. Could all students see whatever information that was presented visually?　　　Ⓨ Ⓝ

10. Did the teacher keep the presentation of new information brief?　　　Ⓨ Ⓝ

11. Did the teacher present complex ideas in "chunks" and provide time for students to demonstrate understanding of one piece before proceeding to the next?　　　Ⓨ Ⓝ

12. Did students learn strategies for acquiring key concepts (minimizing reliance on memory)?　　　Ⓨ Ⓝ

13. Did the teacher give students rubrics so they could evaluate the quality of their work?　　　Ⓨ Ⓝ

In a strong lesson, a "yes" answer is recorded for at least seven of these items.
In an outstanding lesson, a "yes" answer is recorded for at least ten of these items.

Suggested Readings Related to Introducing Content Logically, Clearly, and Concisely

At its core, teaching is communication. Various researchers and authors have explored how teachers communicate more effectively when they introduce content logically, clearly, and concisely. The following articles and books underscore the major ideas presented in this chapter.

Combs, W. E. (2012). *Writer's workshop for the common core: A step-by-step guide.* Larchmont, NY: Eye On Education.

> Many teachers find it difficult to teach writing in a clear, logical, and concise manner. Combs provides a step-by-step approach to teaching writing that makes the complex attainable for a wide range of students.

Cruickshank, D. R. (1985). Applying research on teacher clarity. *Journal of Teacher Education, 35*(4), 44–48.

> Cruickshank emphasizes that logical and clear teaching requires teacher knowledge, planning, and effort. He explains that effective teachers have to "orient and prepare students for what is to be taught; communicate content so that students understand; provide illustrations and examples; demonstrate; . . . teach things in a related step-by-step manner; . . . and provide feedback to students about how well they are doing" (p. 44).

Fendick, F. (1990). *Correlation between teacher clarity of communication and student achievement gain: A meta-analysis.* Doctoral dissertation. Available from ProQuest Dissertation Express. (UMI No. 9115979).

> A variety of auditory factors influence clarity. Fendick stresses the importance of teachers' clarity of speech. Fendick explains that a variety of factors, including lack of volume, lack of expression, vague pronouns, monotonous/dull speech, lack of fluency, and poor grammar can impair clarity and negatively influence students' understanding.

Hattie, J. A. C. (2009). *Visible learning: A synthesis of over 800 meta-analyses relating to achievement.* Abingdon, Oxon: Routledge.

> Instruction can be more concise and effective when teachers guide students in practicing strategies they can use to enhance and monitor their own learning. Hattie found that effective teachers "aim to get students to learn the skills of teaching themselves— to self-regulate their learning" (p. 245). Instead of giving students all of the information, teachers can help students of all ages and ability levels access information, verify answers, and apply information to solve problems.

Marzano, R. J. (2007). *The art and science of teaching: A comprehensive framework for effective instruction.* Alexandria, VA: Association for Supervision and Curriculum Development.

Chapter 2 of Marzano's book describes teaching strategies that are important in helping students acquire and utilize new knowledge. In this chapter, he emphasizes that "learning proceeds more effectively if students receive information in small chunks that are processed immediately" (p. 44).

Marzano, R. J., Pickering, D. J., & Pollock, J. E. (2001). *Classroom instruction that works: Research-based strategies for increasing student achievement.* Alexandria, VA: Association for Supervision and Curriculum Development.

Researchers have explored the ways in which visual prompts can enhance clarity. In Chapter 6 of their book, Marzano, Pickering, and Pollock emphasize the value of nonlinguistic representations (visual aids) in promoting clear understandings. They explain that when teachers engage students in creating various kinds of graphic representations, physical models, or pictures, students not only understand the concepts in greater depth but also recall them much more easily.

Popham, W. J. (2008). *Transformative assessment.* Alexandria, VA: Association for Supervision and Curriculum Development

Popham suggests a four-step strategy for building learning progressions that complements the practices described in the first two chapters of this book. The four steps include "(1) thoroughly understanding the target curriculum aim, (2) identifying all requisite precursory sub-skills and bodies of enabling knowledge, (3) determining whether students' status with respect to each preliminarily identified building block can be measured, and (4) arranging all building blocks in an instructionally defensible sequence" (p. 47).

Rosenshine, B. (2012, Spring). Principles of instruction: Research-based strategies that all teachers should know. *American Educator,* pp. 12–39.

Among the ten instructional principles that Rosenshine discusses in this article is the practice of presenting new material in small steps. Since our working memory can hold only a small amount of information, presenting too much material at once may make it impossible for students to process it. Rosenshine explains that more successful teachers did not overwhelm their students by introducing too much at one time; rather, they taught in small steps and then guided their students in practicing the material. In contrast, the least effective teachers presented an entire lesson and then passed out worksheets.

Saphier, J., Haley-Speca, M. A. & Gower, R. (2008). *The skillful teacher: Building your teaching skills*. Acton, MA: Research for Better Teaching.
    Saphier, Haley-Speca, and Gower insist, "Skillful teachers are clear about what is to be learned, clear about what achievement means, and clear about what they are going to do to help students attain it" (p. 2). Chapter 9 of their book explores a variety of strategies teachers can use to promote the clear and logical presentation of information.

Wiggins, G. P., & McTighe, J. (2005). *Understanding by design* (Expanded 2nd ed.). Upper Saddle River, NJ: Pearson Education, Inc.
    Wiggins and McTighe contend that teachers can increase the likelihood of student understanding by backward mapping: starting with the desired learning outcome and identifying the logical steps that might lead to mastery. This logical approach can lead to strong learning results, even with highly complex academic content.

4

Acquiring and Responding to Evidence of Understanding

In a fourth-grade classroom at Branch Brook School in Newark, New Jersey, students worked busily in small groups pursuing their reading assignment. Each group had the task of reading a novel and creating a book review. Every student had a specific role that was essential to the group's success, so everyone had to be involved. The teacher floated from group to group, listening to student conversations about the important items for inclusion in the review. One student had the important job of asking questions that the book review should address. As the student asked questions, the other students attempted to answer. Students did not always agree, but they had learned to support their answers through the text, providing evidence for their answers from the novel.

When the teacher saw that one student was responding less often than others, the teacher asked the student, "What do you think? Do you agree or disagree? Why?" or some similar question, both to make the student think and to place the student back in the thick of the conversation. If a student had difficulty answering, the teacher probed in a manner that helped the student use prior knowledge, relate, consider alternatives, or otherwise move closer to understanding the important aspects of the novel.

In this case, the teacher was listening to hear what students understood and what they did not understand. It was as if he wanted the novel to come to life in each child's mind with sufficient clarity that the student would be able to see and understand story elements and understand how the author had pursued and accomplished his purpose. The depth and quality of the conversation made it clear that some students had achieved this level of understanding. The teacher, however, wanted every student to demonstrate this level of understanding, either through the conversation among his or her peers or through the teacher's careful probing.

Branch Brook School is in the Newark Public Schools in Newark, New Jersey. The school serves approximately 170 students in grades pre-kindergarten through four. The school won the National Excellence in Urban Education Award in 2010.

■

In high-performing urban schools, teachers seek abundant evidence that students understand the concepts and skills being taught. To promote mastery of a specific concept, teachers frequently check to determine if their students have acquired meaning from the information shared in the prior few minutes. Teachers rarely assume that students understand. Instead, they look for evidence of understanding in oral responses, written responses, or other performances or demonstrations. This checking for understanding occurs with much greater frequency than it does in more typical schools. In typical schools, teachers might ask a few questions at the end of the chapter or lesson. In contrast, teachers in high-performing urban schools ask questions continuously. Also, in typical schools, checking for understanding is often limited to a few students (the ones who raise their hands to respond), whereas in high-performing urban schools, teachers check all or almost all students to ensure that everyone makes progress in mastering the lesson content. Furthermore, in high-performing urban schools, checking for understanding is purposeful and strategic. Teachers do not ask questions simply because the teacher's guide makes the suggestion or because the principal is watching. Instead, teachers check because they want accurate information about students' levels of understanding so they can respond by adjusting instruction accordingly.

Acquiring and responding to evidence of understanding is high-quality formative assessment. It is not an event (like giving a semester test) as much as it is a way of teaching. Great teachers continually want to know if their students are making sense of what they are teaching. These teachers seek oral, written, and nonverbal feedback from their students continuously. Fisher and Frey (2007) explain that teachers can use a wide array of questioning techniques, writing tasks, projects, performances, and tests to acquire high-quality information about what students understand, misunderstand, or have yet to understand. As well, these teachers use the feedback they acquire to refine their teaching, modify their examples, reframe their questions, highlight different connections, and guide students closer to mastery of the content they need to learn. In his article regarding formative assessment, Stiggins (2005) explains that teachers should use assessment to promote better quality teaching and learning. In the schools we studied, we found teachers modeling this type of formative assessment continually, in ways that promoted student mastery.

Frequency of Checking for Understanding

In most classrooms in high-performing urban schools, student voices are heard more frequently than teacher voices. Teachers spend less time presenting. They spend more time trying to determine what students understand. Teachers present new information, but then check almost immediately to determine if students heard, processed, and internalized the information accurately. Continually and persistently, teachers in high-performing schools check: Did this student understand? Does this make sense to her? Can he relate to this? Can she explain this in her own words?

In typical classrooms, teachers might lecture for ten, twenty, thirty minutes or longer before asking students questions. In contrast, in high-performing urban schools, teachers are asking questions every few minutes and in some cases, every few seconds. A teacher at William Dandy Middle School in Fort Lauderdale, Florida (Broward County Public Schools), offered her rationale for her frequent questioning by explaining, "I am assessing all the time. I need to know if my students are with me or not. I don't let them fall behind, not even for a minute."

Often teachers develop systems that allow them to check every student's level of understanding efficiently. For instance, some teachers give students individual white boards and markers and expect them to write responses to a question simultaneously. For example, a teacher might say, "Write on your white board a mathematical sentence that illustrates this story. Don't show your answer until I ask you to do so." Then, at the teacher's signal, everyone raises their white board and shows their work. The teacher can quickly look at every response and determine if all, most, a few, or no students answered correctly. This type of approach challenges all students to respond and allows the teacher to gauge the progress of students who have varying academic strengths and needs.

In some classrooms, teachers acquire evidence of understanding by asking students to respond in unison. In these situations, teachers ask a question and then listen closely for variations in answers. We have also observed teachers listening carefully and noticing which student or students did not respond simultaneously with the group. For example, when the kindergarten teacher at C.E. Rose Elementary in Tucson, Arizona, did not hear every student answer her call for a group response, she said, "I didn't hear Alejandro's row," in a manner that prompted those students to participate fully.

Frequently, teachers will follow up by calling upon students who were slow to answer and asking them to respond individually. Thus, the unison response should be more than a rote drill or a meaningless script. In high-performing urban schools, teachers use unison responses efficiently and effectively to determine that all students understand the information presented.

At Ira Harbison Elementary in San Diego, California (National School District), teachers use electronic clickers as a way of getting quick feedback about students' levels of understanding. Students frequently use their clickers to "vote" for answers that appear on the electronic Smart Board. The technology allows teachers to determine which students answered correctly or incorrectly and adapt their instruction accordingly.

In many classrooms, teachers check for understanding by asking students to write short responses. As students write sentences or paragraphs, teachers rapidly circulate throughout the classroom observing what students are writing. Teachers watch students as they perform, allowing them to immediately see errors in thinking. Often, teachers quickly determine which students understand and which students need additional support.

In high-performing elementary, middle, and high schools, we observed teachers checking for understanding by engaging students in group discussions focused upon the lesson objective. Teachers stimulated discussion with thought-provoking, sometimes controversial, questions and then carefully monitored the discussion that followed. If discussion occurred in small groups, teachers rotated from group to group and listened to determine if students understood the key concepts associated with the lesson objective.

At R. N. Harris Integrated Arts/Core Knowledge School in Durham, North Carolina, a second-grade teacher used games that required students to work in teams in order to answer questions about the history and geography of China. While all students participated in deliberations about the answers to the questions, students took turns writing and reporting their group's answers. As a result, all students were held accountable for demonstrating their learning.

Although teachers in high-performing urban schools use a variety of teaching strategies to acquire evidence of student understanding, the most common method seems to be frequent questioning targeted to individual students. Through their questioning, teachers create a climate in which students know that they must be attentive because there is a high likelihood that in the next moment, the teacher will pose a question that they will be expected to answer.

It is important to note that in high-performing urban schools, teachers do not accept silence as evidence of understanding. Rarely (if ever) in high-performing urban schools did we hear teachers check student understanding by asking, "Any questions?" Instead, teachers asked students to explain what they understood, discuss it, teach it to the student sitting next to them, write a letter to explain the procedure to a friend, draw a diagram, or engage in some other activity that would give the teacher a clear indication of what students understood and what unanswered questions remained.

Well-Distributed Checking for Understanding

In high-performing urban schools, teachers try to ensure that all students have abundant opportunities to respond to questions. They want evidence that each and every student is making progress toward developing deeper levels of understanding. Teachers acquire such evidence through both their question-posing strategies and their careful attention to the responses of each student.

Of course, when teachers use any of the group response strategies described previously, they give all students opportunities to respond. For example, when teachers ask students to solve a problem on their individual white boards, they give every student an opportunity to respond. The teacher can quickly check every student's level of understanding. In a more typical class, a teacher might ask one student at a time to come to the classroom board and solve a problem. While one student responds, other students may disengage. Furthermore, when teachers use such one-student-at-a-time strategies, only a few students might have an opportunity to share. Then, the teacher has little or no information to determine if the other students understand the concept or skill.

In high-performing urban schools, teachers distribute opportunities to respond well even when they do not use group response strategies. Commonly, these teachers call upon students before they raise their hands. In some cases, teachers draw student names randomly to ensure evenly distributed response opportunities. In other classrooms, teachers use a class roster or grade book to help them make sure that all students have opportunities to answer questions. Generally, however, teachers in high-performing urban schools do not restrict their questioning to students who raise their hands and asked to be called upon. Randomly, sequentially, or strategically, they call upon students in a manner that offers all students opportunities to respond. Or, in some classrooms, teachers achieve the same even distribution of response opportunities by allowing students to call upon each other. For instance, in an English class at Kearny School of International Business in San Diego, California, a student answered the teacher's question about the memoir the class was reading, *The Glass Castle*, and then asked another student to offer additional or contradictory evidence from the memoir. Sometimes, the teacher called upon students, and at other times, the teacher allowed students to call upon each other. Clearly, however, she intended to ensure that every student contributed to the conversation.

At Kearny School of International Business, as in other high-performing urban schools, students are not ignored when they sit quietly and passively. The school's principal explained, "Students here are not allowed to sit quietly and fail. That's unacceptable." Instead, all students are expected to participate actively in class discussions. They are challenged to respond to questions in ways that demonstrate their level of understanding.

The thorough distribution of response opportunities in high-performing school classrooms may help explain why certain student populations achieve much better results than are typical. For example, English learners, students with disabilities, or students with behavior challenges are not allowed to sit passively. Teachers engage those students in answering questions at least as much as they engage other students. Students learn that they are expected to learn. Students know that each day, in each class, they will be called upon to participate, engage, and demonstrate their understanding.

Checking for Higher Levels of Understanding

In high-performing urban schools, teachers strive to ensure all students are able to answer questions that require high levels of cognitive ability. All students are expected to learn the lesson objective and demonstrate a depth of knowledge that extends beyond surface-level recall. Thus, teachers will ask many questions that require students to compare, contrast, explain, describe, infer, analyze, and evaluate.

Pushing for higher levels of understanding is not, however, the same as asking questions students find impossible to answer. In high-performing urban schools, teachers work to build student capacity to respond to these challenging questions. For example, teachers may ensure that students first master more basic concepts before they pursue more complex ones. Teachers may pursue lower levels of understanding before asking questions that require deeper levels of cognitive demand.

An important strategy for maximizing student mastery is differentiating the questions students must answer. Students are more likely to invest effort in listening and participating if they know that they will be called upon to answer a question that is challenging, yet targeted to their current level of skill or need. For example, in a kindergarten class at Golden Empire Elementary in Sacramento, California, the teacher gave students turns at blending together three or four letter sounds and then reading the one-syllable word. The teacher prompted each child to say the sounds in the word, blend the sounds together, and then read the word quickly. The students found the task challenging; however, most succeeded on the first try. When the teacher gave Maria a turn, the teacher picked a more difficult one-syllable word and did not prompt Maria to say the sounds first. Maria immediately read the word correctly. Through this small, subtle adaptation of content and process, the teacher acknowledged Maria's ability, gave her an opportunity to practice at a level that was appropriately challenging, and kept Maria highly engaged throughout the lesson.

In many high-performing urban schools, teachers differentiate tasks by the cognitive complexity of the questions they ask, by the amount of time elapsed since the teacher or another student provided information similar to the information requested, or through the details of the prompts provided. For example, a teacher might ask one student to describe a procedure, ask another to explain an application of the procedure to a real-life situation, and then ask another student to discern if there might be another way to approach the problem. In another classroom, a teacher might call upon one student to answer a challenging question, and then call upon a struggling student to answer a very similar question, slightly restated. All of these approaches might address the same objective while providing all students opportunities to advance toward higher levels of understanding.

Observing and Adapting

In high-performing urban schools, teachers check for understanding because they want to know how each student is proceeding toward mastery of the lesson's specific objective. They ask questions to determine which concepts are understood by which students and which concepts have yet to be understood. Therefore, when teachers ask questions, they listen attentively. Similarly, when they ask students to write or demonstrate their understanding, teachers watch closely and notice what students write and do. They want to see students work so they can better understand students' thought processes.

Teachers in high-performing urban schools are eager to learn what students understand and what they may not yet understand. Teachers often probe to validate their assumptions about what students know and do not know. Importantly, teachers keep their specific objective in mind because they want to know how the student is progressing toward mastering the specific concept or skill. For example, if the objective requires students to analyze the findings from an experiment, the teacher may ultimately ask questions that demand analysis of complex information; however, en route to such an objective, the teacher may seek to ensure that students are mastering the details and concepts they will need to perform complex analyses later.

As teachers listen and watch, they respond to students in ways that help students move closer to mastery of the objective. In particular, teachers provide feedback in ways that quickly correct misconceptions and affirm accurate responses. Rather than avoiding public acknowledgement that a given answer is indeed wrong and spending time attempting to elicit a correct response, a teacher might respond, "No, that is incorrect," and then offer the correct answer. The teacher might challenge students to explain why the initial answer was incorrect or why the correct answer makes sense, but the teacher does not leave students guessing about accurate or inaccurate information. Teacher feedback is prompt, clear, and respectful.

Throughout the lesson, teachers continually make decisions about instruction based upon their perceptions of levels of student understanding. In other words, the lesson activities are influenced by feedback received from students. Teachers decide what students might need to understand, see, hear, touch, or experience to advance closer to mastering the lesson objective. Often, teachers might try to adapt their presentation of a concept in a manner that better connects to the interests, backgrounds, learning styles, prior experiences, or culture of the students they serve. (See Chapter 5 for a detailed discussion of this topic.)

In addition to adapting lesson content, teachers might alter the pace of instruction based upon the feedback they garner from students. If student responses indicate high levels of mastery, teachers might accelerate their pace. Conversely, if students are answering incorrectly, teachers might adapt by slowing their progression from one concept to the next.

In addition to making adaptations within lessons, teachers also adapt subsequent lessons based upon the extent of student understanding. In many high-performing urban schools, we observed teachers using end-of-lesson checks or exit tickets to gauge the extent of student understanding. In some cases, the exit ticket was a set of oral responses to teacher questions. In some cases, the exit ticket required students to demonstrate or model a response. In others, the exit ticket prompted a short written response. The exit ticket helped the teacher know how to adapt the plan for the next day's instruction to build upon student levels of understanding. If student responses indicated high levels of mastery of the day's specific objective, the teacher might plan the following lesson to address the next more challenging objective associated with the standard being taught. If exit-ticket responses indicated a lack of understanding, teachers might use the exit ticket to help define specifically what students understood and what they did not understand. Then, the next lesson might be focused in a manner that built upon existing understandings, while addressing the very specific content students still needed to learn.

For example, a teacher might use five subtraction word problems as an exit ticket for her math lesson. Students might respond to each question by writing each subtraction problem and showing their answers on their personal white boards at the teacher's cue. By watching and noting student responses, the teacher might determine that all but three students answered four of the five questions correctly. Also, the teacher might notice that half of the students answered the problem that required regrouping across zeros incorrectly. In response, the teacher might plan to devote the next lesson to word problems that require regrouping across zeros. Additionally, the teacher might plan a focused intervention session with the three students who needed additional assistance.

Adequate Daily Progress for Every Student

While many urban schools have struggled to achieve adequate yearly progress (AYP) in accordance with Title I of the Elementary and Secondary Education Act, all of the schools we studied met and exceeded all AYP criteria in the years prior to their selection for the National Excellence in Urban Education Award. Perhaps part of the secret to their success can be attributed to the manner in which these schools achieved adequate daily progress for each of their students.

In other words, by seeking and acquiring evidence of understanding, teachers in these schools made sure that students made progress each day. Furthermore, these teachers did not ignore the students that some might consider the most difficult to teach. Instead, teachers made sure those students responded to questions that pushed them to engage, learn, grow, and master the content being taught that day. Adequate daily progress added up to adequate yearly progress and beyond as students discovered that they could succeed academically.

What It Is & What It Isn't
Acquiring and Responding to Evidence of Understanding

■ What It Is

Checking to determine students' level of understanding frequently

Example: As the teacher tries to help students understand the relationship between the earth's revolution around the sun and the four seasons, the teacher presents one PowerPoint slide that illustrates the tilt of the earth's axis toward the sun during summer and then asks students a series of questions: Where is it going to be summer in this picture? Why? Where is it going to be winter in this picture? Why? Will the days be longer or shorter in the Northern Hemisphere? Why? Then, the teacher asks one student to stand and act the role of the sun and asks another to hold a Styrofoam model of the earth with a pencil axis. The teacher asks the students to model summer. Then the teacher asks other students the same series of questions. After asking at least a dozen questions, the teacher progresses to the next PowerPoint slide that illustrates the tilt of the earth's axis away from the sun during winter. Then, the teacher poses a similar set of questions.

What It Isn't

Infrequently checking to gauge students' understanding

Example: The teacher shows a PowerPoint presentation intended to explain the relationship between the earth's revolution around the sun and the four seasons. With each PowerPoint slide, the teacher offers a three-minute lecture that discusses issues related to the tilt of the earth's axis, the earth's distance from the sun, and the differential impact on the hemispheres, the equator, and the poles. At the conclusion of the lecture, the teacher asks students to answer questions about the seasons.

■ **What It Is**

Checking each and every student's level of understanding

Example: In a middle school math class, a teacher presents x-y graphs that illustrate hourly wages, hours worked, and bonuses earned. The teacher organizes students into small teams of three and designates each student as Student A, B, or C. The teacher asks the students to work with their teammates to explain what the graph implies about salaries. Then, the teacher asks Student B in each group to stand and explain the graph to their team. Next, the teacher asks each Student A to answer specific questions about data points on the graph (e.g., How much did this person earn and why?). Then, the teacher asks each Student C to explain how the graph would change if either the hourly rate changed or the bonus changed.

What It Isn't

Checking only a few students

Example: In a middle school math class, a teacher presents x-y graphs that illustrate hourly wages, hours worked, and bonuses earned. The teacher presents each graph and asks questions about specific data points, trend lines, and so on. A few students raise their hands or blurt out answers. The teacher calls upon the students who want to participate in the conversation. Other students sit quietly and wait for the period to end.

■ **What It Is**

Checking for higher levels of understanding

Example: As students sit in a circle and read *Charlotte's Web*, the teacher asks a variety of questions intended to promote thinking about cause and effect relationships. For example, the teacher asks, "Why were the animals worried about Wilbur? What did the animals think would happen if Charlotte wrote words over Wilbur's head?" Then, the teacher asks students to share the cause and effect questions that they wrote on sticky notes as they read the chapter. As students read their questions, the teacher guides students in considering first if the question examines cause-effect relationships. Then, the teacher invites students to answer the question using specific evidence from the text.

What It Isn't

Asking questions that require only the recall of facts

Example: As students read *Charlotte's Web*, the teacher asks students multiple questions about details in the story (e.g., Who was Charlotte? Where did Fern live? What was the first word Charlotte wrote in her web?).

■ *What It Is*

Observing students' levels of understanding and adapting instruction accordingly

Example: In Spanish class, the teacher engages students in conjugating the present tense of the verb *hablar* (to speak). While students successfully repeat the conjugation, several students respond incorrectly when the teacher asks them to explain why they need to know how to conjugate the verb. Then, the teacher strays from her planned activity and writes the word *speaks* on the board. She asks the students to generate different sentences that correctly employ the verb. Then, she asks students why none of them offered sentences that started with *I speaks* or *We speaks*. Students laugh and explain that it would not have been proper English. The teacher then explains how verb conjugations in English follow general rules, just as verb conjugations in Spanish follow general rules.

What It Isn't

Ignoring information about student misconceptions

Example: In Spanish class, the teacher engages students in conjugating the present tense of the verb *hablar* (to speak). While students successfully repeat the conjugation, several students respond incorrectly when the teacher asks them to explain why they need to know how to conjugate the verb. The teacher hears the incorrect answers but does not want to take the time to explain. She continues with the conjugation of the next Spanish verb.

Practice Guide Related to Acquiring and Responding to Evidence of Understanding

For information on possible uses of this practice guide, please see pages 5–6 in Chapter 1.

1. During the observation, did the teacher ask students (on average) more than one question for every two minutes observed?   Ⓨ Ⓝ

2. During the observation, did the teacher ask students (on average) more than one question per minute?   Ⓨ Ⓝ

3. Did at least 25 percent of students respond to questions focused upon the objective?   Ⓨ Ⓝ

4. Did at least 50 percent of students respond to questions focused upon the objective?   Ⓨ Ⓝ

5. Did at least 75 percent of students respond to questions focused upon the objective? Y N

6. Did at least 90 percent of students respond to questions focused upon the objective? Y N

7. Did at least 25 percent of the questions asked require students to use higher cognitive skills than recall or memorization? Y N

8. Did at least 50 percent of the questions asked require students to use higher cognitive skills than recall or memorization? Y N

9. Did at least 75 percent of the questions asked require students to use higher cognitive skills than recall or memorization? Y N

10. Did at least 25 percent of students explain/discuss objective-related ideas with peers? Y N

11. Did at least 50 percent of students explain/discuss objective-related ideas with peers? Y N

12. Did at least 75 percent of students explain/discuss objective-related ideas with peers? Y N

13. Did at least 90 percent of students explain/discuss objective-related ideas with peers? Y N

14. Were most questions answered correctly by students? Y N

15. Did the teacher notice and respond appropriately to each student's correct or incorrect answer? Y N

16. If the teacher provided students opportunities for unison responses, did the teacher notice and respond appropriately when students did not respond? Y N

17. If the teacher provided students opportunities to respond in writing, did the teacher observe students as they wrote? Y N

18. Did the teacher alter strategies, examples, or methods when students did not understand? Y N

19. Did the teacher end the lesson by checking to determine students' levels of understanding?   Ⓨ   Ⓝ

20. Were all students attentive and engaged throughout the lesson? (If not, which students were not and why?)   Ⓨ   Ⓝ

_____

_____

_____

In a strong lesson, a "yes" answer is recorded for at least ten of these items.
In an outstanding lesson, a "yes" answer is recorded for at least fifteen of these items.

Suggested Readings Related to Acquiring and Responding to Evidence of Understanding

Focusing instruction upon mastery requires that teachers have a way of monitoring students' learning and adjusting instruction along the way. The body of research on formative assessment and checking for understanding offers rich information about the history, purpose, strategies, and desired outcomes of gathering and responding to evidence of student understanding. The following articles and books provide support for and examples of the key practices outlined in this chapter.

Black, P., & Wiliam, D. (1998). Inside the black box: Raising standards through classroom assessment. *Phi Delta Kappan, 80*(2), 139–149.

For this seminal article, Black and Wiliam reviewed the research to date and found substantial evidence that formative assessment is an essential component of classroom practice and, when used well, produces significant achievement gains. As a result of this review, the authors conclude that instruction and formative assessment are inseparable and that "opportunities for students to express their understanding should be designed into any piece of teaching." Black and Wiliam also articulate the potential of teacher/student discussions to increase students' understanding of their own thinking. Yet, the authors contend that teachers' selection of questions, predetermined notions of correct responses, and propensity to answer their own questions after a short wait time were likely barriers to student participation and divergent thinking.

Blackburn, B. R. (2008). *Rigor is not a four-letter word.* Larchmont, NY: Eye On Education.

> The quality of a teacher's questions influences the quality of information teachers acquire about student understanding. Blackburn offers practical suggestions for improving the rigor of the questions teachers pose.

Brookhart, S. M. (2008). *How to give effective feedback to your students.* Alexandria, VA: Association for Supervision and Curriculum Development.

> Providing descriptive feedback to students about their progress toward mastery is a central component of formative assessment. Brookhart's book offers teachers guidelines for delivering effective feedback. She outlines important elements of feedback content and strategy while sharing practical suggestions that include the kinds of feedback best suited for various content areas.

Corno, L. (2008). On teaching adaptively. *Educational Psychologist, 43*(3), 161–173.

> In general, Corno describes adaptive teaching as responding to learners as they work, reading student signals to diagnose needs on the fly, and tapping into previous experience with students to respond productively. Corno found that adaptive teachers differentiated instruction in a way that provided advanced and weaker students with opportunities to be challenged and supported in class. They did so by creating a "middle teaching ground" at the intersection of different levels, keeping most students at the center by "adjusting teaching to learners and learners to teaching."

Fisher, D., & Frey, N. (2007). *Checking for understanding: Formative assessment techniques for your classroom.* Alexandria, VA: Association for Supervision and Curriculum Development.

> Fisher and Frey explain the nature of checking for understanding and why it is important in influencing learning results. Also, they offer practical guidance on how teachers can check for understanding through their use of oral language, questions, writing, projects and performances, and common assessments.

Hattie, J., & Timperly, H. (2007). The power of feedback. *Review of Educational Research, 77*(1), 81–112.

> Feedback is one of the most powerful influences on learning and achievement, whether positive or negative. Its power is frequently acknowledged, but surprisingly few studies have systematically investigated its meaning. This article provides a conceptual analysis of feedback and reviews the evidence related to its impact on

learning and achievement. The authors advance a feedback model that identifies the particular properties and circumstances that make it effective and suggest ways feedback can be used to enhance its effectiveness in classrooms.

Nuthall, G. (2005). The cultural myths and realities of classroom teaching and learning: A personal journey. *Teachers College Record, 107*(5), 895–934.

Nuthall, reflecting upon forty-five years of experience in and research on teaching, provides a detailed account of the ritualized practices and supporting beliefs that have challenged meaningful reform in teaching and learning. Perhaps most troubling as it relates to formative assessment is the persistent belief that telling and teaching are the same thing; that what works in face-to-face conversation will work with a class of twenty to thirty students; and that attending only to head nodding, eye contact, and facial expression will provide sufficient evidence of understanding. Consequently, as Nuthall explains, "Teachers depend on the responses of a small number of key students as indicators and remain ignorant of what most of the class knows and understands" (p. 920).

Popham, W. J. (2008). *Transformative assessment.* Alexandria, VA: Association for Supervision and Curriculum Development.

Chapter 3 of Popham's book focuses on how teachers use formative assessment to make decisions about whether they need to adjust their current teaching or what they will do next instructionally. In particular, Popham describes the following four steps that a teacher must take to make effective instructional adjustments: (1) identify the specific points in the learning progression when the adjustment decisions should be made; (2) select the assessment procedures; (3) determine the level of performance that would trigger an instructional adjustment; and (4) make the instructional change.

Roberts, T., & Billings, L. (2012). *Teaching critical thinking: Using seminars for 21st century literacy.* Larchmont, NY: Eye On Education.

When teachers acquire and respond to evidence of understanding, they systematically check all students and they ensure that students are being asked high-quality questions that require critical thinking. Roberts and Billings offer practical suggestions for both practices as they describe techniques that teachers can use in seminar settings.

Ross, P., & Gibson, S. A. (2010). Exploring a conceptual framework for expert noticing during literacy instruction. *Literacy Research and Instruction, 49,* 175–193.

A growing body of research sheds light on what effective teachers notice during instruction. In their article, Ross and Gibson contend that instructional decision making depends upon the capacity of teachers to attend to and make sense of instructional situations. Expert noticing, as compared to less expert noticing, seems to involve more detailed hypothesizing, greater elaboration, and the capacity to identify pivotal events during instruction.

Stiggins, R. (2005). From formative assessment to assessment for learning: A path to success in standards-based schools. *Phi Delta Kappan, 87*(4), 324–328.

In this article, Stiggins revisits the traditional role of assessment in schools, accounts for the resurgence of interest in formative assessment, and offers a new approach that places learning at the center of assessment. This approach, argues Stiggins, rests on the premise that when students have continual access to feedback about their learning, they can set goals, watch their progress, and develop confidence that their continued success is possible.

5

Connecting with Student Interests, Backgrounds, Cultures, and Prior Knowledge

As usual, the conversations in this sophomore English class at Lawndale High School near Los Angeles, California, were intense. Groups of three or four students (mostly Latino and African American) were leaning in, talking to each other with an air of urgency. Everyone was on task. The teacher floated from group to group, offering suggestions, but the students clearly were self-directed. Each group had the task of rewriting a scene from Shakespeare's *King Lear*. The students had to rewrite their scene in a manner that would be easily and completely understood by any of their peers. Students were using their notes from the prior class conversation, as well as the well-worn pages of the play, to help them confer, discuss, and even argue about the appropriate language that would best communicate the scene's meaning to their peers.

A student in one group read from Act 4, Scene 1, "As flies to wanton boys are we to the gods. They kill us for their sport."

Instantly, another explained, "The dude is bummed out. They blinded him."

"Yeah, but how should we rewrite his line?" prompted another student. "Kids aren't going to get what 'flies to wanton boys' means."

The student who had read the line offered a suggestion. "How about if we rewrite it to say, 'Life is messed up!'"

"That's good," one of the students offered, "but he needs to say something about how he's blaming the gods."

After thinking for a minute, a student suggested, "Life is messed up! The gods are just playin' us!"

The others nodded in agreement. They wrote the line and went to the next paragraph in the play.

> *Lawndale High School is in the Centinela Valley Union High School District near Los Angeles, California. The school serves approximately 1,550 students in grades nine through twelve. The school won the National Excellence in Urban Education Award in 2009.*

■

Teachers in high-performing urban schools help more students achieve mastery, at least in part, because they teach concepts in ways that resonate with their students. Often in collaboration with their colleagues, teachers ask themselves, "How can I get *my* students to understand this challenging concept?" As a result, teachers are more likely to produce lessons that connect with the interests, backgrounds, cultures, and prior knowledge of their students.

Building Connections

The teacher at Lawndale High School in the aforementioned example could have just as easily taught Shakespeare in a traditional manner, but would his students have been just as likely to understand, internalize, or remember? In high-performing urban schools, we observed lessons in which teachers made new concepts seem familiar to their students. At Dreamkeeper's Academy in Norfolk, Virginia, we saw elementary students learning and practicing Spanish vocabulary by performing skits in which students acted out restaurant scenes and ordered familiar foods. Similarly, at Henderson Middle School in Richmond, Virginia, teachers employed a variety of visual, hands-on, and cooperative instructional methods to make sure their students succeeded. They regularly used learning games, manipulatives, technology, flow charts, hands-on projects, and graphic organizers that helped students connect their prior knowledge and experiences to the content their teachers were endeavoring to teach. At Southside Elementary in Miami, Florida, every lesson centered upon the use of an artifact. These physical objects helped students understand complex and unfamiliar concepts and ideas.

Gay (2010) argues that underachieving students from various racial/ethnic groups would achieve much more if teachers taught to and through their students' personal and cultural strengths, prior accomplishments, and experiences. In the award-winning schools we studied, we saw many examples of this type of instruction.

At several schools (e.g., R.N. Harris Integrated Arts in Durham, North Carolina; Muller Elementary in Tampa, Florida; Hambrick Middle School in Houston, Texas [Aldine Independent School District]; and Cecil Parker Elementary in Mount Vernon, New York), we saw innovative uses of art, music, dance, physical education, and drama to reinforce important academic concepts related to mathematics, reading, science, writing, and social studies. Teachers cleverly tapped into student interests and backgrounds in ways that helped students relate to and understand important academic concepts. Teachers used art to help students learn geometric concepts related to symmetry, rotation, and parallelism. They used sheet music to reinforce concepts and skills related to fractions. They used games played during physical education to help students practice multiplication facts.

While it is important to note that not every lesson was innovative or inspiring, at the high-performing schools we visited, we saw many examples of teachers presenting challenging academic content in ways that helped students relate the concepts and skills to their prior knowledge, interests, backgrounds, and cultures.

Teachers shared that the development of intriguing, powerful lessons took time and energy. Teachers shared that they worked in collaboration with their peers to build lessons that would create "aha" experiences in which students made sense of new concepts by connecting the new ideas to things they had experienced or things that interested or excited them. Often, teachers used collaboration times (e.g., department meetings, grade-level planning meetings, professional learning communities) to pool their best ideas and generate lessons that students would perceive as interesting, relevant, or even exciting.

Rarely did we see teachers relying solely upon textbooks or workbooks to teach challenging concepts or skills. In fact, we saw far fewer worksheets in high-performing schools in comparison with what we typically see in struggling urban schools. In contrast, we saw many more manipulatives, we heard many more real-life examples, and we heard many more student discussions about the connections between the academic standards they were learning and their interests, backgrounds, and concerns.

A math teacher at Franklin Towne Charter High in Philadelphia, Pennsylvania, explained, "If I just have them [my students] do what's in the textbook, they probably won't understand. I've got to figure out how to make it come to life for them. Somehow, I've got to make it real to them." Many teachers in the high-performing urban schools we studied evidenced a similar commitment.

Perhaps, it should go without saying that it is difficult to "connect" with someone you do not know. In order to create lessons that connect with students' backgrounds, interests, culture, and prior knowledge, teachers must know their students. Teachers need to know what students find interesting and exciting. They need to know how students spend their time and what piques their interests. They need to know what students are most eager to read and what they stay up late to play on their technological devices.

Teachers in high-performing urban schools take the time needed to learn about their students. They do so because they care (see Chapter 8). But also, they do so because they want to learn how to best tailor learning experiences in ways that spark the interests of their students.

Not Simply for the Sake of "Interesting"

It is important to note that in high-performing schools, lessons are rarely designed or pursued simply because they are likely to be interesting to students or because they are likely to relate to students' backgrounds or cultures. In contrast, teachers are keenly focused on getting students to master key academic concepts and skills. Almost always, these concepts and skills are rooted in state and district standards. Teachers approach the teaching of these concepts and skills in ways that relate to students' interests, backgrounds, cultures, and prior knowledge.

The first priority is teaching the content students must learn in order to succeed academically and in life. A second consideration is how teachers might deliver the content in ways that resonate with their students. In other words, teachers are not likely to teach a unit on hip-hop music just because students would find it intriguing. They would, however, be more likely to use hip-hop music to teach a state standard that focused on the use of rhyme and meter in poetry.

Teachers were focused on the same challenging academic standards that we see addressed in more typical schools. In fact, in the high-performing schools we visited, teachers spent more time and energy focused upon rigorous academic standards than is typical for urban schools. They also, however, approached those rigorous standards in ways that integrated the interests, backgrounds, cultures, and prior knowledge of their students.

Assumption of Student Ability

Teachers at the schools we studied evidenced a strong belief that their students could learn challenging concepts. We heard several teachers echo the sentiment of a teacher at Escontrias Elementary in El Paso, Texas, who explained, "We know they [our students] can achieve anything. We just have to find a way to get them to learn it."

In fact, the assumption that students can achieve at high levels may be essential. It is difficult to imagine teachers working diligently to find more effective ways to teach a skill if they assume their students are destined to fail or incapable of learning. Unfortunately, some teachers may perceive that they have conclusive evidence that their students are not likely to succeed at learning rigorous content. Sometimes, these teachers possess multiple years of experience observing their students fail. Apart from placating their administrators, they see no reason to try different instructional approaches, because they already know the outcome will be failure and frustration.

In contrast, educators in high-performing urban schools have learned to share effective lesson strategies that are tailored to the strengths, interests, and backgrounds of their students. One teacher's success in ensuring that students master a concept in biology leads another to apply a similar strategy in the teaching of a chemistry principle. Successes snowball, creating a culture where teachers assume that their students can achieve academic excellence if they create the appropriate learning opportunity, taking best advantage of their students' strengths, culture, interests, and prior knowledge.

Ongoing Checking to Ensure Connection

A teacher at William Dandy Middle School in Fort Lauderdale, Florida, explained that generating interesting, engaging lessons is not easy. "Sometimes, we think that we've come up with a lesson that students will relate to. We'll try it out and we'll see that students really aren't getting it. So, we sometimes have to stop in the middle of a lesson and switch it up."

Even when teachers believe they have planned lessons that will connect with their students' interests, backgrounds, cultures, and prior knowledge, they observe closely to determine if students understand key concepts and ideas. If students do not understand, teachers modify their approaches and use different examples that are more likely to make the content come to life for students. As teachers observe and find students struggling, they build in additional examples, aids, steps, or supports to help increase student mastery. Often those supports are ideas that better connect to students' backgrounds, interests, and prior knowledge.

At the same time, as teachers observe and find students excelling, they build in additional opportunities to extend concepts and deepen understanding. For example, students who understood how to use square linoleum tiles to measure the area of their rectangular classroom might find it exciting and challenging to calculate the amount of ceramic tile they would need to surround their dream house swimming pool.

In the highest performing schools, teachers are constantly trying to enrich student learning by generating small and large activities that offer students greater opportunities to apply the concepts that are central to the teacher's lesson. For example, at Horace Mann Elementary and Columbus Elementary in Glendale, California, teachers give "must do" and "may do" assignments. The "may do" assignments extend upon the essentials and provide students greater opportunities to apply what they have learned to real situations. At the World of Inquiry School in Rochester, New York, students engage in exciting projects that allow them to see how the core academic concepts they learn are connected to things they experience in life. At Mueller Charter School in Chula Vista, California, students use the local nature center as their laboratory, learning about ecological issues that influence their community. At Southside Elementary in Miami, Florida, the various museums in the downtown area surrounding the school are major resources that teachers use to make science, social studies, reading, mathematics, art, and other subjects come to life.

What It Is & What It Isn't
Connecting with Student Interests, Backgrounds, Cultures, and Prior Knowledge

■ What It Is

Planning lessons that will teach important academic objectives by including activities, examples, or resources to which students are likely to relate

Example: A biology teacher engages students in a discussion of people they have encountered who have various genetic disorders. They talk about the prevalence rate of each type of disorder for the general population and for specific racial/ethnic groups in the population. Then, the teacher assigns various small groups of students the task of finding the genetic source of a specific disorder. Students must create presentations that explain the genetic cause of the disorder and illustrate the genetic dysfunction. They must explain how one might predict the likelihood that various pairs of parents would have a child with the disorder.

What It Isn't

Assuming students will relate to and understand abstract presentations of information

Example: A biology teacher has students read Chapter 4 of the biology book, which focuses on genetics. After students read the chapter, the teacher provides a lecture that reiterates the major concepts presented in the chapter.

■ What It Is

Getting to know one's students

Example: A middle school teacher stands at the classroom door and greets students as they come into his science class. Before he asks one student to remove the headphones from his ears, he asks the student what song is playing. Quietly, he asks another student how his evening went. Then, as students are sitting down, he asks, "Who likes their music loud?" When almost all of the students roar affirmatively, he asks, "How loud is loud? How do you know how loud you like it?" Students can't figure out how to respond. Then, the teacher explains that by the end of the class period, the students will know how to measure volume and pitch and assess risks to hearing.

What It Isn't

Not taking time to get to know one's students

Example: The middle school teacher science teacher presents a lesson on sound volume and frequency by covering a worksheet that displays the typical decibel range of various types of noises and the sound frequency range of various symphonic instruments.

■ *What It Is*

Pursuing interesting or fun lessons because they relate to important academic objectives

Example: A teacher is trying to help students practice the challenging vocabulary they are learning in economics. The teacher engages students in creating Jeopardy-like questions/answers that require knowledge of the economics vocabulary learned over the past several weeks. After the questions/answers are developed, the students divide into teams and play the game using the questions/answers they created.

What It Isn't

Pursuing interesting or fun lessons that will not help students learn important academic objectives

Example: A teacher decides that students need a break from the challenging economics curriculum and decides to engage the class in a game of Jeopardy. Immediately, the students are excited as they divide themselves into teams and begin responding to the various items across the different answer categories.

■ *What It Is*

Checking in an ongoing manner to ensure that connections are effective

Example: A teacher decides to make reading class more interesting by engaging students in comparing/contrasting the story they are reading to a popular television show. Before the teacher gives the assignment, she asks students questions about the television show and learns that few students have seen it. She then modifies her plan by asking students to discuss television shows that have similar story lines to the story they are reading. As almost all students relate story lines from one particular television show, the teacher gives an assignment asking students to compare and contrast a story line from that particular show with the story they are reading.

What It Isn't

Assuming that lessons intended to create a connection with students will actually succeed in doing so

Example: A teacher decides to make reading class more interesting by engaging students in comparing/contrasting the story they are reading to a popular television show. Students begin work on the assignment; however, only a few of the students have ever seen the new television show. The teacher assumes that the lack of quality responses is due to students' difficulties understanding the concepts *compare* and *contrast*.

Practice Guide Related to Connecting with Student Interests, Backgrounds, Cultures, and Prior Knowledge

For information on possible uses of this practice guide, please see pages 5–6 in Chapter 1.

1. Did the lesson build upon students' interests/backgrounds? (Y) (N)

2. Did the lesson build upon students' prior knowledge? (Y) (N)

3. Did the teacher explain concepts in ways that helped students relate? (Y) (N)

4. Did at least 90 percent of the students listen actively throughout the lesson? (Y) (N)

5. Did at least 25 percent of the students demonstrate enthusiasm related to the lesson? (Y) (N)

6. At least 50 percent? (Y) (N)

7. At least 75 percent? (Y) (N)

8. If students did not understand, did the teacher modify examples? (Y) (N)

9. If students did not understand, did the teacher scaffold concepts to increase understanding? (Y) (N)

10. If students mastered concepts early, did the teacher offer a higher level of challenge? (Y) (N)

In a strong lesson, a "yes" answer is recorded for at least five of these items.
In an outstanding lesson, a "yes" answer is recorded for at least seven of these items.

Suggested Readings Related to Connecting with Student Interests, Backgrounds, Cultures, and Prior Knowledge

Breaux, E., & Magee, M. B. (2010). *How the best teachers differentiate instruction*. Larchmont, NY: Eye On Education.

In order to connect with students' interests, backgrounds, cultures, and prior knowledge, teachers must know their students. Then, teachers must know how to differentiate instruction in ways that adapt appropriately and effectively. Breaux and Magee offer practical suggestions for getting to know students' learning strengths and needs and adapting instruction accordingly.

Delpit, L. (2005). *Other people's children: Cultural conflict in the classroom* (2nd ed.). New York: The New Press.

It is difficult to connect with children you do not know. In this book, Lisa Delpit explores the importance of teachers' knowing the cultures of the students they serve, so that they might provide instruction that is likely to be effective.

Gay, G. (2010). *Culturally responsive teaching: Theory, research, and practice* (2nd ed.). New York: Teachers College Press.

This book describes the research that addresses the power of culturally responsive pedagogy. Specifically, Gay examines four aspects of culturally responsive teaching: caring, communication, curriculum, and instruction. Each of these aspects has important implications for teachers who endeavor to maximize learning results for diverse populations of students.

Germain-McCarthy, Y., & Owens, K. (2005). *Mathematics and multi-ethnic students: Exemplary practices.* Larchmont, NY: Eye On Education.

The authors explain that "many students today perceive mathematics to be a bunch of numbers that plug into formulas to solve problems. More often than not, the problems they are asked to solve are not their problems, nor do they come close to something they are interested in pursuing" (p. 5). This book offers practical suggestions for teaching mathematics in ways that connect with the backgrounds and cultures of diverse groups of students.

Howard, T. (2001). Powerful pedagogy for African American students: A case study of four teachers. *Urban Education, 36*(2), 179–202.

Howard examined the pedagogical practices of four highly effective elementary teachers working with African American students in urban settings. Twenty-one nominators (school district administrators, principals, teachers, parents, and civic leaders) identified teachers whose pedagogical practices were deemed effective in contributing to the academic and social development of African American students. The four teachers consistently used culturally responsive pedagogy, designing lessons that featured instructional strategies that helped students connect the challenging academic content being presented with their backgrounds, cultures, and experiences.

Irvine, J. J. (2003). *Educating teachers for diversity: Seeing with a cultural eye.* New York: Teachers College Press.

In this article, Irvine emphasizes that culturally relevant pedagogy was not easy. She explains that teachers cannot acquire this pedagogical proficiency by simply attending a workshop or learning about diversity. Unfortunately, school administrators and teacher educators give insufficient attention to the challenges associated with helping teachers develop these pedagogical skills.

Ladson-Billings, G. (2009). *The dreamkeepers: Successful teachers for African American children* (2nd ed.). San Francisco: Jossey-Bass.

Gloria Ladson-Billings studied teachers who successfully educated African American children. In her book, she explores and describes how classrooms worked when teachers operated through a paradigm that was relevant to, sensitive to, and responsive to the cultural differences of students.

Rajagopal, K. (2011). *Create success: Unlocking the potential of urban students.* Alexandria, VA: Association for Supervision and Curriculum Development.

In this book, a California Teacher of the Year describes the CREATE model, which includes Culturally responsive instruction, Rigorous expectations and rewards, Essentials-focused planning, Assessing for mastery during class, Test models, and Extra one-on-one tutoring for struggling students. The book offers a host of practical examples for teaching in ways that connect with students' interests, backgrounds, and cultures.

Reyes, P., Scribner, J. D., & Scribner, A. P. (1999). *Lessons from high-performing Hispanic schools.* New York: Teachers College Press.

The authors identified Texas schools near the U.S.–Mexico border that achieved impressive results for Latino students and English learners. They specifically acknowledge the ways in which educators in high-performing schools valued students' first language and their home culture. As well, they report evidence that teachers in high-performing, diverse schools tailored lessons in ways that connected to the backgrounds, cultures, prior knowledge, and experiences of the students they served.

Tomlinson, C. A. (1999). *The differentiated classroom: Responding to the needs of all learners.* Alexandria, VA: Association for Supervision and Curriculum Development.

This book presents a framework for differentiating classroom instruction that emphasizes students' prior knowledge, interests, and learning profiles. Starting with a focus on student differences, the author provides practical examples of ways in which teachers can structure their classrooms so all students are likely to succeed.

6

Building Student Vocabulary

Colorful pictures and neatly printed words covered the walls of classrooms in this inner-city, Los Angeles school in the Montebello Unified School District. Barren wall spaces were rare, as students had literally thousands of reminders of the words they had learned throughout the year in various subject areas. In one first-grade classroom, the teacher pointed to a picture on the wall:

"Maria, what is this?"

"It is a picture of snow," Maria correctly answered.

"Yes, and what do we know about snow, Miguel?"

"Cold?" Miguel shyly answered, as if he hoped he had pulled the correct word from his small English vocabulary.

"In a complete sentence, please," insisted the teacher.

"Snow is cold. Snow is very cold," Miguel responded with a little more confidence.

"Excellent! And what else do you know about snow, Javier?"

"Snow falls from the sky in snowflakes."

"That's right! Snow falls from the sky in snowflakes. In summer?" the teacher challenged, pointing at Eva.

"No," Eva giggled and explained, "snow falls from the sky in winter."

"Are you sure about that, Manuel? I don't remember seeing any snow here in Los Angeles this winter," the teacher challenged again.

"Not here. In the mountains," Manuel explained.

"In a sentence," the teacher reminded.

"It doesn't snow here in Los Angeles. It snows in the mountains in winter."

Montebello Gardens Elementary School is in the Montebello Unified School District in Los Angeles, California. The school serves three hundred students in grades kindergarten through four. The school won the National Excellence in Urban Education Award in 2009.

■

In high-performing urban schools, teachers help students master the vocabulary that serves as a gatekeeper to understanding challenging academic content. The gates of understanding swing open when students are fluent users of essential vocabulary related to the objective teachers want students to learn. Conversely, the gates of understanding tend to remain closed when students cannot converse using key words and concepts. The only students who reach a deep level of understanding are those who have integrated the key lesson vocabulary into their personal vocabularies. In every subject area (including mathematics, science, English, social studies, and others), students are likely to achieve mastery only when they have mastered the key lesson vocabulary.

For example, in the science lesson described at the beginning of Chapter 2, the teacher at Horace Mann Dual Language Academy worked to ensure that every student was comfortable with the Spanish words for *volcano*, *magma*, *eruption*, and *pressure*. She checked in various ways to ensure that students were comfortable speaking and using these words in proper context. If students had not been able to speak and use the lesson's critical vocabulary, they would have been less likely to accurately explain the relationships between the concepts. They would have been less likely to ask pertinent questions. Similarly, they would have been less likely to advance to the more challenging concepts the teacher planned to teach in subsequent lessons.

Pre-Identification of Critical Vocabulary

In many of the lessons we observed in high-performing urban schools, teachers had pre-identified these gatekeeper vocabulary words associated with each lesson. In particular, they focused upon words that conveyed important concepts, functions, and relationships associated with the lesson objective they wanted students to master. In many cases, we saw the critical vocabulary posted next to the objective the teacher wanted students to master. For example, in a ninth-grade algebra lesson at MacArthur High School in Houston, Texas (Aldine Independent School District), a teacher had written the words *intercept* and *slope* on cards and placed them prominently on the board at the beginning of the lesson. She engaged students in describing common usages of the terms. Students responded by discussing interceptions in football or soccer. They also discussed the notion of mountain slopes. Next, the teacher pushed students to discuss how those common usages might apply to mathematics and to their specific lesson on graphing linear equations. Through these conversations, she helped students gain familiarity with the terms. They were better prepared to participate in instruction that required them to use these concepts.

Teachers at Signal Hill Elementary in Long Beach, California, carefully pre-identified important vocabulary words associated with the lessons they intended to teach. The teachers explained that this was essential to ensure the academic success of the many English learners who attended their school. The teachers explained, "Many students who speak English at home have never or rarely heard some of the academic vocabulary that is important in our lessons. These words may be just as foreign to them as they are to our English learners."

At several high-performing urban schools, teachers pre-identify critical vocabulary during grade-level or department planning meetings. For example, at Lauderbach, Montgomery, and Otay Elementary Schools in Chula Vista, California, teachers meet in grade-level teams to determine how they will ensure that all students master the challenging academic objectives they intend to teach. During these meetings, teachers ask themselves, "What words will our students need to know and understand in order to master this concept?" The critical vocabulary words are recorded in planning team minutes and lessons are designed to ensure that students learn those words.

Building "Ownership" of Critical Vocabulary

It is important to note that teachers in high-performing urban schools were very deliberate in ensuring that all students had multiple opportunities to practice using the essential lesson vocabulary. Teachers did not merely post words and ask students to find definitions in a glossary or dictionary, copy words, or copy sentences. Instead, we saw many examples of teachers making sure that students practiced the words in meaningful sentences. In a manner consistent with the practices described by Marzano and Pickering (2005), we heard students explaining to their peers how important vocabulary words were similar or different in their meaning or usage. We heard students helping each other use different forms of key vocabulary words, as they built fluency with new vocabulary.

In the first-grade classroom at Montebello Gardens (discussed at the beginning of this chapter), the teacher made sure that her students did more than see or read the vocabulary. She made sure that students *owned* the vocabulary. By asking many questions and requiring students to answer in original sentences that utilized the central vocabulary, the teacher promoted student fluency and confidence. This teacher, like many teachers in high-performing schools, listened attentively and provided useful feedback to help students use the vocabulary accurately.

Similarly, in a violin lesson at KIPP Adelante Academy in San Diego, California, the middle school music teacher asked, "What does *adagio* mean?" When a student answered correctly, the teacher exclaimed, "Yes, that's right! So what is *allegro*?" When a student answered correctly, the teacher played short measures on the violin and after each musical phrase asked, "So what is the tempo of that?" Students answered in unison with the words *adagio* or *allegro.* Then, the teacher asked students, "Play this line adagio. Play this line allegro," and students demonstrated the concepts through the use of their violins. The teacher made sure that students had a working understanding of these words prior to proceeding with the lesson.

Also at KIPP Adelante Academy, a science teacher led students in a game that required students to memorize hand signals for vocabulary words associated with a lesson on weather. Students worked in groups to practice the hand signals for *condensation, hurricane, evaporation, tornado,* and a few other words. The hand signals provided clues about the meaning of each word. The game engaged students in hearing, saying, and making hand movements associated with each word. By the time the game ended, students were well prepared to discuss the weather-related concepts in greater depth because they were familiar with the vocabulary.

In a science lesson at MacArthur High School, a teacher asked students to explain to their lab partners what *viscosity* was. The teacher had already explained the term, but he wanted students to explain the term in their own words. Next, he asked them to identify liquids that were more or less viscous and explain why. The activity required students to speak the key vocabulary word. As the teacher circulated throughout the room, he prompted students to use the vocabulary even more. "Yes," he affirmed to one group of students and then asked, "So, what does that mean about honey?" A student responded, "Honey is more viscous than water."

At MC^2 STEM High School in Cleveland, Ohio, a teacher introduced the terms *compression* and *tension* as they related to bridge engineering. The teacher demonstrated how compression points worked as students began to build their own bridges. As the teacher moved among the groups of students, he asked them to explain their designs in terms of compression points, tension, and other vocabulary terms related to bridge engineering. Students had to practice the vocabulary the teacher wanted them to understand.

In some schools, we observed teachers using sentence frames or paragraph frames to help students become more confident in using key lesson vocabulary. For example, at Bonham Elementary in the Dallas (Texas) Independent School District, a third-grade teacher engaged small groups of students in generating answers to the sentence frame, "I inferred that the main character was _____ because _____ ." Students had to use the word *inferred*, but the sentence frame helped them do so accurately. Every student in the class used the word *infer* (in its various forms) multiple times during the lesson. The activity led students to understand and utilize the concept of inferences at a level that often eludes much older students.

At Columbus Elementary in Glendale, California, instructional aides were trained to help small groups of students learn and practice critical vocabulary words. In one classroom, while the teacher worked with a group of students on a guided reading activity, the instructional aide helped a different group practice key vocabulary words. The aide reminded the students about the meaning of a word and challenged students to engage in dialogue, using the word frequently.

For example, an aide presented the word *astonished* and then asked students, "How would you feel if a kid brought an elephant to school?" Students immediately answered that they would be astonished, so the aide asked, "Why would you be astonished?" Each student in the group answered the question, using the vocabulary word correctly.

Usable Word Walls

To promote the continued use of important vocabulary words, many teachers in high-performing urban schools posted the vocabulary words students had learned. These word walls were referred to often throughout lessons. Teachers often acknowledged students for using posted vocabulary correctly. In many classrooms, like the first-grade classroom at Montebello, word walls became giant glossaries that helped students remember and practice the words they had learned. The word walls were also valuable tools for improving student writing.

Word walls were not just room decorations. Instead, they were tools that teachers used to prompt students to remember and encourage them to use important lesson vocabulary. At the same time, word walls were often implicit celebrations of the vocabulary students had learned. At MacArthur High, important vocabulary words were hung in each corridor as reminders of the concepts students had learned.

Original Writing

In high-performing urban schools, we saw a strong emphasis on writing. In all curricular areas, students were expected to write in ways that explained their understanding of important ideas and concepts. In many schools, teachers expected students to practice new vocabulary in writing activities. As students became more familiar with vocabulary, teachers required students to write paragraphs, letters, stories, and essays in which they utilized the key vocabulary in original sentences. For example, at Golden Empire Elementary in Sacramento, California, we saw student writing that explained the distinctions between animal classifications. At Charles Lunsford Elementary in Rochester, New York, we saw student writing that explained the procedure for solving multi-step math problems. At Hambrick Middle School in Houston, Texas, students wrote explanations of the different roles and responsibilities of the three branches of the federal government. In all of these and many other examples, writing activities gave students the opportunity to practice using the vocabulary they had discussed during the lesson.

What It Is&What It Isn't
Building Student Vocabulary

■ *What It Is*

Pre-identifying the vocabulary students must master in order to achieve the lesson objective

Example: A statistics teacher considers the vocabulary students need to master in order to have a deep understanding of the concept of standard deviation. The teacher identifies a list of critical terms, including some that students should have already learned (e.g., mean, median, data set) and some new words (e.g., frequency, standard, deviation, normal curve, distribution). The teacher plans a lesson to ensure that students have multiple opportunities to demonstrate that they understand these words before she introduces the concept of standard deviation.

What It Isn't

Starting a lesson without considering which vocabulary words might become stumbling blocks that impede mastery

Example: A statistics teacher introduces a lesson on standard deviation. The teacher wants students to understand and be able to use the concept of standard deviation. The teacher methodically shares with students the procedure for calculating the standard deviation of a data set. To help make the lesson interesting, the teacher uses data sets that are familiar to the students. Learning, however, is limited because students are not conversant with several of the terms the teacher uses, including *distribution*, *deviation*, and *frequency*.

■ *What It Is*

Building "ownership" of critical vocabulary

Example: The teacher shares with students a handcrafted, felt board model of an animal cell and explains that the students will learn about the various parts of the cell, their names, and their functions. The teacher removes one felt piece from the board and explains, "These are mitochondria. Everyone say 'mitochondria.'" The teacher explains why mitochondria are important to the cell. Then she hands the felt piece to a student and asks, "What are you holding?" When the student answers "mitochondria," the teacher asks about their function. The teacher invites the student to give the mitochondria to another student, and explain what he or she is giving. The teacher then asks the second student similar questions about the mitochondria. Then the teacher asks all the students what would happen to the animal if all of the mitochondria were removed. Students work in pairs to generate a complete answer with strong rationale. Then, the teacher calls upon several students to share their responses before she moves to the next organelle on the felt board.

What It Isn't

Engaging students in routine vocabulary activities that do not require students to use new vocabulary frequently

Example: In a lesson on the structure of animal cells, the teacher has students use the glossary of their biology text to find the definitions of several components of animal cells. Students must write the definitions on worksheets and create posters showing an animal cell with the appropriately labeled parts.

■ What It Is

Using word walls as teaching tools

Example: A third-grade teacher maintains a word wall that includes vocabulary from each story the class has read. The word wall is divided into five large sections: nouns, verbs, adjectives, adverbs, and other parts of speech. When a new story is introduced, students engage in discussions of the selected vocabulary words. Students must place the word in the correct word-wall section in alphabetical order. Working in teams, students develop "model sentences" that reflect various uses of each vocabulary word. A few of the model sentences get posted next to the appropriate vocabulary word on the word wall. Students receive bonus points when they use any word-wall words in their writing assignments if the words are used in an appropriate context and spelled correctly. At the end of each reading lesson, the teacher engages students in a random review of one word from each section of the word wall.

What It Isn't

Having word walls as wall coverings

Example: A third-grade reading teacher maintains a word wall that includes vocabulary from each story the class has read. Before a story is read, the teacher posts five or six vocabulary words onto the word wall. When the story is introduced, the teacher carefully discusses each of the vocabulary words and engages students in discussion of the words.

■ *What It Is*

Engaging students in writing original pieces to practice the use of new vocabulary

Example: As an opening activity for each class, a government teacher requires students to write a paragraph concerning a concept discussed in the previous day's lesson. Each writing prompt asks students to write about a problem or an issue associated with the main vocabulary concept introduced. For example, after a lesson on bicameral legislatures, an opening activity requires students to write a paragraph that explains why bicameral legislative governments might generate gridlock.

What It Isn't

Engaging students in copying words or sentences that use new vocabulary

Example: A government teacher requires students to copy a set of words that relate to the day's lesson on the legislative branch of government. Students must also copy a set of sentences that correspond to each vocabulary word. Students keep the words and sentences in their government class journals.

Practice Guide Related to Building Student Vocabulary

For information on possible uses of this practice guide, please see pages 5–6 in Chapter 1.

1. Did the teacher pre-identify and present the vocabulary essential to mastering the lesson objective? (Y) (N)

2. Did the teacher provide examples of the use of lesson vocabulary that students were likely to understand? (Y) (N)

3. Did the teacher post the lesson's key vocabulary? (Y) (N)

4. Did at least 50 percent of students read/say the essential vocabulary words? (Y) (N)

5. At least 75 percent? (Y) (N)

6. Could every student asked read and explain the meaning of the key vocabulary? (Y) (N)

7. Did the teacher hear at least 25 percent of the students using the key lesson vocabulary in original sentences? (Y) (N)

8. At least 50 percent? (Y) (N)

9. At least 75 percent? (Y) (N)

10. Did the teacher acknowledge students' correct usage of key lesson vocabulary from the current or previous lessons? (Y) (N)

12. Did the teacher respond appropriately to student errors in using the lesson vocabulary? (Y) (N)

13. Did the teacher provide students opportunities to write using the key vocabulary in context? (Y) (N)

In a strong lesson, a "yes" answer is recorded for at least six of these items.
In an outstanding lesson, a "yes" answer is recorded for at least nine of these items.

Suggested Readings Related to Building Student Vocabulary

As students come to own critical vocabulary, they unlock the gates to challenging academic content. A significant body of research on vocabulary instruction reveals the importance of providing students, of all ages, robust opportunities to experience words, both through explicit teaching and through independent encounters. These books and articles provide practical and empirical examples of high-quality vocabulary instruction, echoing the examples described in this chapter.

Arechiga, D. (2012). *Reaching English language learners in every classroom: Energizers for teaching and learning.* Larchmont, NY: Eye On Education.

  Several chapters in Arechiga's book provide suggestions that relate to building student vocabulary. In particular, Chapter 7 emphasizes the importance of getting students to talk and practice using new vocabulary. As well, the chapter offers a variety of suggestions to promote student practice of critical vocabulary.

Beck, I. L., & McKeown, M.G., (2007). Increasing young low-income children's oral vocabulary repertoires through rich and focused instruction. *Elementary School Journal, 107*(3), 251–271.

  This article reports on studies conducted with kindergarten and first-grade children from a low-achieving elementary school. In one study, the students' regular classroom teacher provided two groups of students differing amounts of instruction on advanced vocabulary found in children's trade books that are typically read aloud. For one group, the instruction went well beyond what is typically required in vocabulary instruction and assessment, requiring students to make decisions about the appropriateness of contexts for newly learned words, develop uses for new words, and explain why uses made or did not make sense. The vocabulary gains for kindergarten and first-grade children, who received more instruction, were twice as large. The findings demonstrate that children as young as kindergarteners and first graders can add sophisticated words to their vocabularies. Further, the findings reveal that additional robust instruction brings about better results.

Beck, I. L, McKeown, M. G., & Kucan, L. (2002). *Bringing words to life: Robust vocabulary instruction*. New York: Guilford Press.
 This book provides a research-based framework, along with practical strategies, for student vocabulary development. Authors emphasize the power of instruction that offers rich information about words and their uses, enhancing students' language comprehension and production. Teachers will find key-word selection strategies; methods for developing explanations of new words; and suggestions for facilitating students' thinking about words, use of words, and noticing of new words both within and outside the classroom.

Blachowicz, C. L. Z., & Fisher, P. (2000). Vocabulary instruction. In M. L. Kamil, P. B. Mosenthal, P. D. Pearson, & R. Barr (Eds.) *Handbook of reading research*. (Vol. 3, pp. 502–523). Mahwah, NJ: Erlbaum.
 The chapter chronicles the history of research on vocabulary instruction, from the early decades of educational research forward.

Dougherty Stahl, K. A. & Bravo, M.A. (2010). Contemporary classroom vocabulary assessment for content areas. *Reading Teacher, 63*(7), 566–578.
 This article presents a variety of research-based content area vocabulary assessments, demonstrating how teachers can develop vocabulary assessments based on their own curricular needs. Dougherty Stahl and Bravo encourage teachers to assume an assertive stance in developing their own vocabulary assessments.

Fisher, D. (2007). Creating a schoolwide vocabulary initiative in an urban high school. *Journal of Education for Students Placed at Risk, 12*(3), 337–337.
 In an effort to improve student achievement at an urban high school, teachers and administrators developed a five-part, school-wide plan for building student vocabulary. Fisher followed the school's efforts over four years, chronicling the ways in which teachers read to their students, provided students increased

opportunities to read independently, developed content-specific vocabulary instruction, taught students academic words, and focused on five words each week, containing a common prefix, suffix, or root. Across four years, student achievement in vocabulary and reading comprehension improved in significant ways, both on reading assessments and state achievement tests.

Graves, M. F. (2006). *The vocabulary book: Learning and instruction*. New York: Teachers College Press.

    This text presents a comprehensive plan for vocabulary instruction from kindergarten through high school. Graves illustrates his research-based approach by means of detailed classroom examples and strategies that teachers can readily apply. The four-part plan includes rich and varied language experiences, teaching individual words, teaching word-learning strategies, and fostering word consciousness.

Hardwick-Ivey, A.R. (2008). Vocabulary in action: Strategies for turning students into wordsmiths. *English Journal, 97*(4), 56–61.

    High school teacher Amy R. Hardwick-Ivey describes specific strategies for increasing students' understanding of the nuances of language and their confidence in using language well.

Kelley, J. G., Lesaux, N. K., Kieffer, M. J., & Faller, S. E. (2010). Effective academic vocabulary instruction in the urban middle school. *Reading Teacher, 64*(1), 5–14.

    To address the needs of struggling readers, including language minority students and their native English-speaking classmates, these scholars developed and evaluated an academic language program in partnership with an urban school district characterized by linguistic and socioeconomic diversity. Kelley and colleagues sought to determine if regular, systematic academic vocabulary instruction, delivered in mainstream classrooms, effectively bolstered students' reading comprehension skills. Findings underscore the strengths of multifaceted vocabulary instruction that targets high-utility academic words; covers a small number of these words in depth; anchors the words in engaging text; incorporates multiple, planned exposures to each word; and balances direct instruction in word meanings with teaching word-learning strategies.

Marzano, R. J., & Pickering, D. J. (2005). *Building academic vocabulary: Teacher's manual*. Alexandria, VA: Association for Supervision and Curriculum Development.

    This manual describes a six-step approach for teaching 7,923 of the most important vocabulary terms across eleven subjects and four grade-level intervals. The six-step approach is designed to help students develop understanding of the terms they are taught.

Nagy, W. E. (1988). *Teaching vocabulary to improve reading comprehension.* Newark, DE: International Reading Association.

Nagy describes research-based methods of vocabulary instruction that effectively improve reading comprehension. He provides detailed descriptions of instructional strategies that employ these methods. The book further suggests that although reading significantly increases vocabulary, significant vocabulary growth results from both explicit instruction and incidental encounters with words.

7

Promoting Successful Practice

In a third-grade classroom at Horace Mann Elementary School in Glendale, California, the objective read, "Today, I will learn to order numbers." The teacher read the objective and asked, "What does it mean to order numbers?"

"It means to put them in order," offered one child.

"What if someone doesn't know what 'order' means? How would you explain what it means to order numbers?"

Another student suggested, "It means to put the smallest first, then the next bigger one, then the next, until you're done."

"Yes," the teacher affirmed. "That's one meaning. Putting numbers in order can mean placing them from least to greatest. Is there another way of putting them in order?"

"Well, you could switch them from greatest to least," proposed another student.

"Absolutely! That's another way of ordering numbers, from greatest to least. Today, you're going to show me that you can order numbers from least to greatest and from greatest to least. First, I need someone to remind us what *least* means?"

"It means the smallest," answered a student.

"That's right. And, what does *greatest* mean?" queried the teacher.

"It means the biggest," answered another child.

The teacher quickly reminded students about a strategy for comparing the size of three-digit numbers. She demonstrated the strategy with the help of a document camera.

"Look. I have these three numbers: 329, 347, and 315. I need to put them in order from the greatest to the least. Let's see. Where should I start?"

"With the hundreds place?" offered one student.

"Why would I start there?" asked the teacher.

"Because you want to find which one is biggest, so you need to start with the biggest place value."

"Yes. That makes sense," the teacher affirmed, as she underlined the numeral in the hundred's place in all three numbers. "But, that didn't help me much because all of the numbers have a three in the hundred's place."

"So, go to the ten's place," suggested another student.

"Why?" asked the teacher, looking as if she really needed help in understanding.

"Because it's the next biggest place value after the hundreds," answered a student.

The teacher continued to model the strategy while asking students questions at each step. Finally, she had the three numbers placed in the proper sequence and every student had participated in answering at least one question about the process.

"Now, I want you to work with your partner and show me that you know how to order these three numbers from greatest to least." The teacher projected three three-digit numerals through the document camera. Students worked in pairs and recorded their answers on individual white boards. While the students worked, the teacher quickly circulated around the room, determining which students understood and which ones did not.

After a few minutes, the teacher asked everyone to display their answers. Almost all of the pairs answered correctly. She asked students (including those who answered incorrectly) to explain why the correct answer was accurate. One student who answered incorrectly on his white board explained the rationale for the correct answer and explained how he and his partner made an error in the process.

The teacher repeated the process by asking students to order three more three-digit numbers. This time, however, she specified that she wanted students to sequence them from least to greatest. "What are you going to do differently this time?" she asked.

"We've got to find the smallest and put it first," responded a student.

"That's right!" the teacher affirmed and encouraged students to proceed in pairs again, writing their answers on their white boards.

This time, all of the students answered correctly. Again, she asked students to explain their responses. Then, she asked students to practice individually by ordering two sets of three numbers from least to greatest and ordering two sets of three numbers from greatest to least. While students worked individually, the teacher continued to circulate and monitor each child's progress.

> *Horace Mann Elementary is in the Glendale Unified School District in Glendale, California. The school serves approximately 720 students in grades kindergarten through five. The school won the National Excellence in Urban Education Award in 2010.*

■

In high-performing urban schools, teachers ensure that students have at least a moderate understanding of a concept before they ask students to perform the task independently. Generally, students are not asked to practice what they have not learned. In more typical schools, students are often pushed to work independently on tasks that they are ill prepared to pursue. As a result, in more typical schools, students often spend hours practicing incorrect strategies, algorithms, and processes. The misunderstandings, after they have been practiced to perfection, are difficult to correct.

Guided Practice

In high-performing urban schools, teachers take time to guide students through practice activities. As they guide, teachers help make sure students attend to the proper issues and understand the rationale for their actions. In the third-grade class from Horace Mann Elementary, described at the beginning of this chapter, the teacher was not satisfied to hear students offer the correct answer. She wanted to hear students explain why each step made sense.

In high-performing elementary, middle, and high schools, we observed teachers meticulously preparing students to work independently with high rates of success. For example, at Franklin Towne Charter High School in Philadelphia, Pennsylvania, an algebra teacher gave every student in the classroom at least two opportunities to explain parts of the quadratic equation and answer questions about the equation's meaning before she allowed students to open their text books and answer similar questions independently. At William Dandy Middle School in Fort Lauderdale, Florida, science teachers required students to use the graphic organizers they created in small groups to explain the concepts they had learned about genetics. The teacher listened carefully as students explained their graphic organizers to each other. When the teacher was confident that students could explain orally, the teacher gave students a short quiz addressing the same concepts. Similarly, at Louisa May Alcott Elementary in Cleveland, Ohio, primary-grade reading teachers ensured that every student decoded the words in the story correctly (multiple times) before they asked students to read the story independently. Marzano (2010) refers to examples such as these as "structured practice." He explains that the practice was structured to "maximize students' success rates" (p. 80).

In more typical classrooms, we often observe teachers providing small amounts of modeling or demonstrating, then offering little or no guided practice. Large percentages of the class period tend to be devoted to independent practice activities during which large percentages of students struggle. In contrast, in these high-performing urban schools, we saw teachers engaging in more modeling or demonstrating and substantially more guided practice. Students were allowed to practice independently only when the teacher had seen evidence that most or all students possessed the knowledge or skill necessary to proceed successfully.

Teachers worked to ensure that students understood key concepts, and they also worked to ensure that students understood key directions prior to allowing students to work independently. Often teachers asked several students to give detailed explanations of assignment directions. For example, a teacher at Dreamkeepers Academy in Norfolk, Virginia, asked her students, "What will you need to do in order to write this report? What will you have to do first?"

Quickly, she called upon a student who did not have his hand raised.

"First, we have to complete the concept map," the student answered correctly.

"How are you going to do that?" the teacher asked, pointing to another child.

"We're going to get information about the different kinds of rock from our chapter and show it on the concept map?" the student answered and asked simultaneously.

The teacher continued to probe. She asked various students to explain what information they were going to collect, how they were going to display the information, and how they were going to use the concept map to organize their report. It quickly became obvious that students knew how to proceed in a manner that would allow them to complete the assignment successfully.

As a result of this kind of checking, almost all students were able to proceed with assignments with minimal or no teacher assistance. Little or no time was wasted with students trying to figure out how they should begin or what they should do. While this type of checking took more time than simply asking, "Any questions?" teachers saved time that would have otherwise been spent on reexplaining directions or redirecting off-task students.

Guided Struggle

As teachers endeavor to help students learn challenging academic content (such as that required by Common Core State Standards), teachers should expect that students will struggle to understand. A complete absence of struggle might signal that difficult aspects of a concept or skill are not being addressed. As the principal of Whitefoord Elementary in Atlanta, Georgia, explained,

> If all of the children are able to answer all of the questions, there is something wrong—they're not learning new information. I want to make sure the lesson is rigorous enough that some of the information [the teacher] is giving is *new* information, and that [students] are making connections, but I'm concerned if they can answer every single thing and process and digest everything the teacher is giving.

In high-performing urban schools, teachers are masterful at guiding students through difficult concepts. Teachers ask questions, raise issues, and pose challenges that lead students from what they know to what they need to know in order to understand challenging concepts. Instruction of this caliber requires planning. At many high-performing urban schools, such as Highland Elementary in Silver Spring, Maryland, and Otay Elementary in Chula Vista, California, teachers work in teams to deliberately plan how they will guide students to understand difficult concepts. They plan what questions they will ask, and they anticipate the correct and incorrect answers students will provide. They consider how they will use both correct and incorrect answers to lead students to more complete understandings of the concepts they endeavor to teach.

Monitoring Independent Work

In high-performing urban schools, even when students are given independent work, teachers monitor carefully to ensure students are practicing successfully. Typically, we saw teachers looking over students' shoulders, inspecting their work, and checking to make sure students were answering correctly. Students were not allowed to practice repeatedly in an incorrect manner. For example, when a teacher determined that an individual student misunderstood an important aspect of the lesson, the teacher provided immediate assistance. When the teacher surmised that a few students were perplexed or confounded by the concept, the teacher immediately called together the struggling students and provided additional instruction, while other students continued to work independently. On the other hand, if all students were making significant errors, the teacher might abruptly stop the independent work and immediately reteach the concept, using the observed student errors as teaching tools.

Building Student Capacity to Self-Monitor

In high-performing schools, often, teachers equip students with strategies for checking their independent work. By providing students with rubrics, scoring guides, or similar tools, students can self-assess and determine that they are "on target" as they pursue mastery. Students are more likely to maximize their effort when they know they are performing at a level that will earn a strong grade and ensure their mastery of the concept or skill. Simultaneously, students are more likely to ask for focused assistance when a rubric or scoring guide helps them determine that they have not learned a key concept or skill well.

At several high-performing schools, teachers made extensive use of rubrics to help students evaluate their work. For example, at Branch Brook Elementary in Newark, New Jersey, students knew precisely what they needed to do as they worked to "Strive for a 5" in the school's writing program. Detailed rubrics helped students evaluate their work while they were writing. Students could self-correct in a timely manner. Also, students could use the rubrics to evaluate their writing when they completed assignments. In some classes, students took pride in predicting their scores because they understood the rubrics and used them well.

Providing Independent Work (Including Homework) Worth Completing

Independent practice (including homework) is designed to give students meaningful opportunities to practice concepts and skills they have learned. It should not be boring, meaningless repetition. Throughout our observations of high-performing urban schools, we did not see endless seatwork or thick packets of worksheets. Independent practice was focused upon the specific objective the teacher wanted students to master. Independent practice was long enough to confirm that students had truly acquired mastery, yet it was short enough and interesting enough to sustain a high level of student engagement.

Teachers, parents, and students reported that homework was regularly assigned, completed, graded, and returned. Students perceived that homework provided them an opportunity to show how much they had learned. Neither students nor parents tended to perceive that homework was drudgery. Students in high-performing urban schools reported that they succeeded in completing homework regularly. "Yes, we get homework, but it's not too hard and not too easy. You don't have to be a genius to finish your homework," a student at Franklin Towne Charter High School in Philadelphia, Pennsylvania, explained. A parent at Golden Empire Elementary in Sacramento, California, described the differences between homework her child received at Golden Empire and homework the child had received at another school. She remarked,

> At the other school, my child got less homework, but it took him longer to do it. Often, I had to spend a lot of time teaching the math work he needed in order to do the assignment. Here [at Golden Empire], he gets more homework, but he's able to finish it by himself with almost no help from me. Even the math, he's able to do pretty quickly by himself.

In these high-performing urban schools, students perceived their ability to complete homework as evidence that they were smart, talented, and capable. For example, at Lemay Elementary in Los Angeles, California, a child remarked, "The homework is pretty hard, but it's good that they are pushing us . . . we're learning a lot more.

In high-performing urban schools, teachers tend to assign homework that students can complete accurately and independently. For most students, homework becomes a positive opportunity to practice and demonstrate their academic progress. This means that some teachers may differentiate homework assignments. Students who have demonstrated a higher level of mastery might receive more challenging assignments than other students.

What It Is & *What It Isn't*
Promoting Successful Practice

■ *What It Is*

Guiding students as they learn and practice new concepts and skills

Example: A kindergarten teacher works to get children to retell the major events of a story in proper sequence. The teacher reads the story once and then leads the students in discussing the important events in the story. Students have difficulty ascertaining which events were important. The teacher explains that one way to decide if an event was important is to determine if the ending might have been different if the event did not occur. As students mention various events, the teacher helps them use this decision rule in deciding if the event was important. The teacher reads the story a second time and asks students to raise their hands when they hear the teacher mention one of the important events they had discussed. As students identify the important events, the teacher hands children large hand-drawn picture cards that represent each event. The teacher asks students to explain which major events came before and after each event discussed. The teacher models and directs students to practice describing the various events in complete sentences. When the story is finished, the teacher asks all of the students with picture cards to stand up and organize themselves in proper sequence. The students who do not have picture cards are asked to check to be sure the pictures are in the proper sequence. Individual students are then asked to share their major events in proper sequence.

What It Isn't

Quickly pushing students to work independently

Example: A kindergarten teacher works to get children to retell the major events of a story in proper sequence. The teacher reads the story to the students and notes the important events. The teacher discusses the order in which the events occurred, using words like *first*, *second*, *third*, and *last*. Then, the teacher sends students back to their seats to color pictures that represent the major events in the story. Students must then cut out the pictures and paste them on construction paper in the proper sequence.

■ *What It Is*

Guiding students in ways that help them through the struggling necessary to understand challenging concepts

A fifth-grade teacher works to build her students' understanding of multiplying a whole number by a decimal. The teacher writes a problem on the board (512 × 0.25) and asks students what the problem means. Students read the problem accurately; however, the teacher asks students to explain more precisely what the problem means. As students struggle, the teacher asks, "What is 25 hundredths?" When students do not respond, she asks, "Is 25 hundredths larger or smaller than 1?" Several students answer, "Smaller," prompting the teacher to ask, "How much smaller? Talk to your shoulder partner and decide." After students have discussed the issue, the teacher asks one student, who explains that 25 hundredths is a lot smaller than 1 because 25 hundredths is really like 25 cents out of a dollar. "Good!" the teacher exclaims. "So, if you multiply 512 by a number smaller than 1, will the product be larger than 512 or smaller than 512?" Students decide that the product should be a lot smaller than 512. Then the teacher explains that because one of the factors is smaller than 1, one way they can check to make sure that their answer is reasonable is to check to see if the product is considerably smaller than 512. Then, the teacher asks students to explain how they would multiply 512 and 25. Several students explain the algorithm, one step at a time. Frequently, the teacher asks, "Why?" when a student explains a step. The students explain well because of their prior instruction. When students have finished the problem and arrive at a product, the teacher asks a student, "Is this a reasonable answer to the problem 512 × 0.25?" The student answers, "No." The teacher asks another student, "Why?" The student explains that the product is far more than 512. Then, the teacher asks if they did something wrong in calculating. One student explains that they did not do anything wrong. They simply multiplied 512 × 25. They did not multiply 512 × 0.25. The teacher reminds the students of the importance of place value as they multiply two whole numbers. She then explains how they can account for the place value of decimals in factors when they generate a product. Using the simple procedure of counting digits to the right of the decimal, the teacher helps students find the place for the decimal in the product. Then she asks, "Why does that procedure make sense? Talk with your partner." Some students note that the product is now smaller than 512, suggesting that they actually multiplied by a number smaller than 1. Others suggest that if you multiply by a hundredth, the number generated through the algorithm has to be divisible by 100.

What It Isn't

Presenting the easy concepts and allowing students to struggle independently with the more difficult concepts

Example: A fifth-grade teacher works to build her students' understanding of multiplying a whole number by a decimal. The teacher writes a problem on the board (512 × 0.25) and asks students to copy it. Then, the teacher demonstrates how to solve the problem using a common multiplication algorithm. As the teacher moves through the problem, she occasionally asks, "What's the next step?" The same two students answer each time, while others remain silent. After the multiplication is finished, the teacher points to the second factor and asks, "How many digits are to the right of the decimal point up here?" The same students correctly respond, "Two." Then the teacher explains that there must be two digits to the right of the decimal in the product. The teacher explains, "See this is easy. You already know how to do this because you know how to multiply. You just have to remember to count the number of digits to the right of the decimal in the factors and make sure you have the same number of digits to the right of the decimal in the product." Then, the teacher assigns items one through twenty in the textbook. Students work on those independently; however, some students struggle. None of the students correctly answers items nineteen and twenty: the two "Think Big Questions." These questions ask students to explain in a short narrative response why their answers to the first two problems (items one and two) are logical and reasonable.

■ *What It Is*

Monitoring student performance as students complete independent work

Example: After teaching his seventh-grade students how some authors use precise verbs to influence the mood of a story, the teacher asks students to annotate a passage and note the mood created/influenced by the author's choice of verbs. After giving the assignment, the teacher circulates and observes students working. The teacher notes that most students are performing well; however, three students are missing important examples of verbs that influence mood. Also, the three students are making annotations about words that are not verbs. The teacher quietly asks these three students to join him at his desk. While the other students continue to work independently, the teacher guides the three students through the assignment.

What It Isn't

Assigning independent work without monitoring student performance

Example: After teaching his seventh-grade students how some authors use precise verbs to influence the mood of a story, the teacher asks students to annotate a passage and note the mood created/influenced by the author's choice of verbs. After giving the assignment, the teacher returns to his desk and begins correcting last night's homework papers.

■ *What It Is*

Building students' capacity to monitor their own progress in completing assignments well

Example: A seventh-grade social studies teacher requires students to write a paper that compares and contrasts life in the Middle Ages with life during the Renaissance. The teacher guides the students in creating Venn diagrams that illustrate the ways in which life was similar and different during these two time periods. Before students begin the writing assignment, the teacher passes out four unmarked, non-identifiable sample papers for this assignment from students in prior years. In small groups, the students critique the papers and discuss what makes them interesting and informative. Through the students' critique, the teacher guides the students in creating a rubric for their assignment. Once the rubric is created, the teacher explains how she will use the rubric to grade student papers. Then, the teacher asks students to discuss how they can use the rubric to help them create outstanding papers.

What It Isn't

Assuming that students have the capacity to monitor their own progress in completing assignments well

Example: A seventh-grade social studies teacher requires students to write a paper that compares and contrasts life in the Middle Ages with life during the Renaissance. After spending a class period discussing each era, students begin working independently to complete the assignment while the teacher works to respond to e-mail requests from the district office. She directs the students to approach her desk if they have questions.

■ What It Is

Providing students independent work they are likely to perceive as interesting and/or worth completing

Example: After a lesson on converting fractions to percentages and decimals, a teacher gives every student a copy of a newspaper clipping, including the current batting statistics (number of at bats, number of hits, and batting averages) for all members of the local professional baseball team. For homework, students are required to select one player and determine what the player's batting average would be if the player successfully hit during the next five, ten, twenty, and fifty at bats. The teacher engages students in a discussion of how they could go about making such a calculation. Students are encouraged to write down the necessary steps in the process. Then, the teacher asks various students to read a step and explain the rationale for each one. When the teacher is convinced that students know how to proceed, they are dismissed.

What It Isn't

Providing students "busywork" or assignments they are likely to perceive as either repetitive and dull or far too difficult to complete successfully

Example: After a lesson on converting fractions to percentages and decimals, a teacher assigns, as homework, page 128 from the math book. The page includes thirty problems that require students to convert fractions into percentages or decimals and one "Think Big Question" that requires students to read and answer a word problem, requiring the conversion of fractions to percentages and decimals. Immediately, several more capable students groan, whispering to their neighbors about how boring it will be to complete thirty-one uninteresting problems. In contrast, a less capable student sighs and frowns, writing on the bottom of her paper, so her neighbor can see, "I don't even know how to start the first one."

Practice Guide Related to Promoting Successful Practice

For information on possible uses of this practice guide, please see pages 5–6 in Chapter 1.

1. Did the teacher check at least 25 percent of the students to ensure they understood the concept before allowing independent practice? Ⓨ Ⓝ

2. At least 50 percent? Ⓨ Ⓝ

3. At least 75 percent? Ⓨ Ⓝ

4. Prior to giving students independent work, did the teacher check to ensure that students had developed a depth of understanding of key concepts? Ⓨ Ⓝ

5. Prior to giving students independent work, did the teacher check to ensure that students understood the directions? Ⓨ Ⓝ

6. Did students learn strategies for checking their work and assessing their mastery? Ⓨ Ⓝ

7. Did the teacher monitor independent practice to ensure student mastery? Ⓨ Ⓝ

8. Did the teacher provide individual assistance when needed? Ⓨ Ⓝ

9. Did the teacher work with small groups of students when needed? Ⓨ Ⓝ

10. If several students made serious errors in independent practice, did the teacher stop and reteach? Ⓨ Ⓝ

11. If students worked independently, did at least 80 percent get at least 80 percent of the task correct? Ⓨ Ⓝ

12. Prior to giving homework, did the teacher ensure that students   were likely to be able to complete the assignment successfully?

In a strong lesson, a "yes" answer is recorded for at least six of these items.
In an outstanding lesson, a "yes" answer is recorded for at least nine of these items.

Suggested Readings Related to Promoting Successful Practice

Hattie, J. A. C. (2009). *Visible learning: A synthesis of over 800 meta-analyses relating to achievement.* Abingdon, Oxon: Routledge.

Hattie reports that deliberative practice had a substantial effect on student learning results. Hattie emphasizes that practice was most effective when teachers were able to increase the rate of correct academic responses until mastery was achieved. He stresses that this type of practice was not dull and repetitive drill. Instead, findings point to the importance of providing context to facilitate learning transfer, aiming toward deeper and conceptual understandings, and providing opportunities to practice over several days.

Hill, J. D., & Flynn, K. M. (2006). *Classroom instruction that works with English language learners.* Alexandria, VA: Association for Supervision and Curriculum Development.

Building upon the framework provided by Marzano, Pickering, and Pollock (2001), this book examines strategies for improving the instruction of English language learners. Chapter 8 focuses specifically on issues related to homework and practice. Hill and Flynn emphasize that practice activities (including homework) should be differentiated to address student learning needs and strengths and language abilities. As well, they encourage teachers to utilize concrete, nonlinguistic examples; include opportunities for students to ask questions and discuss assignments orally; receive native language support; and receive modified or additional instruction.

Kellogg, R. T., & Whiteford, A. P. (2009). Training advanced writing skills: The case for deliberate practice. *Educational Psychologist, 44*(4), 250–266.

Drawing from the field of cognitive psychology, this article describes the importance of deliberate practice in teaching advanced writing skills. In writing, as in any complex task, learners progress through an early cognitive stage to an intermediate associative stage and then finally into an autonomous stage; however, students are not likely to reach the autonomous stage without extensive deliberate practice. In particular, this means that students are likely to learn to write well only if they spend considerable time writing, with the benefit of quality feedback.

Marzano, R. J. (2010). *The art and science of teaching: A comprehensive framework for effective instruction.* Alexandria, VA: Association for Supervision and Curriculum Development.

Marzano found that practice and homework had substantial effect sizes on student learning results. He emphasizes that practice activities (including homework) should relate directly and explicitly to identified learning goals, should be calibrated to the right difficulty level so students can complete assignments independently, and should be structured to ensure high completion rates.

Rosenshine, B. (1983). Teaching functions in instructional programs. *The Elementary School Journal, 83*(4), 335–351.

Rosenshine analyzed several major studies of effective teaching and determined that "successful learning requires a large amount of successful practice" (p. 337). Rosenshine determined, however, that certain teacher behaviors influenced the extent to which practice was likely to be successful. For instance, Rosenshine found that initial student practice activities should include frequent checking for understanding. Students who were taught well during guided instruction were more likely to succeed at independent practice. When teachers moved around and interacted with students during seatwork, student engagement in seatwork increased. Also, Rosenshine found that cooperative learning activities could be powerful tools for helping students practice successfully.

Saphier, J., Haley-Speca, M. A., & Gower, R. (2008). *The skillful teacher: Building your teaching skills.* Acton, MA: Research for Better Teaching.

In Chapter 10 of their book, Saphier, Haley-Speca, and Gower discuss the importance of the degree of guidance provided to students as they practice new skills. In general, the authors explain that "guidance should be high with new tasks and withdrawn gradually with demonstrated student proficiency" (p. 231). This may often require the differentiation of support based upon student strengths and needs.

8

Making Students Feel Valued and Capable

A group of fourteen sixth-, seventh-, and eighth-grade students gathered in the library at William Dandy Middle School in Fort Lauderdale, Florida. The researcher posed the simple question, "Is this a good place to be a student?" Without hesitation, several students responded immediately, "Yeah, this is a great school."

"So what makes this a great school?" the researcher asked.

"The teachers here care about us," one student offered.

"It's the teachers," another affirmed. "They really want you to succeed. The teachers here care about you."

As the other students nodded their agreement, the researcher asked, "How do you know the teachers care? What makes you think they care about you?"

"They treat us with respect," an older boy offered.

"That's right. They always give us respect," elaborated another.

"Yeah, they give us respect, even when we don't deserve it," a previously silent student explained.

"But, they don't let you get away with stuff," the older student emphasized. "They expect you to do your work. They expect you to follow the rules. But, they treat with you respect."

"They definitely expect you to do your work," a seventh-grade girl confirmed. "And, they don't give us baby work. I get work that's harder than my brother gets. And he's in eleventh grade."

"Is that a good thing?" the researcher probed.

"Yeah!" several students exclaimed. "It's good because they [the teachers] want you to succeed. They want you to be able to go to college and be somebody."

"And it's good because they make you want to work hard," another student articulated.

"How do they do that?" the researcher probed. "How do they make you want to work hard?"

After a pause, one student explained, "They care enough to help us succeed."

Another contributed, "They don't give up on us. They think we're smart. That makes you want to work hard. I don't want to let my teachers down."

William Dandy Middle School is in the Broward County School District in Fort Lauderdale, Florida. The school serves approximately one thousand students in grades six through eight. The school won the National Excellence in Urban Education Award in 2008 and again in 2012.

■

Scheurich (1998) studied schools that had strong academic results for children of color and children from low-income families. He determined that educators in those schools established caring, loving, and respectful environments in which students were expected to achieve at high levels. Similarly, in every high-performing school we studied, students emphasized that their teachers care sincerely about them and their academic success. We believe that almost all teachers care about their students; however, student interviews suggest that students in high-performing urban schools are much more likely to perceive that their teachers care about them and value them. The perception of caring, or lack thereof, influences student motivation and behavior. Somehow, teachers in these schools convince students that the adults in the school value and respect them. Somehow, students become convinced that their teachers are committed to helping them succeed in school and in life. A variety of factors seem to contribute to students' perceptions that teachers care.

Caring Enough to Demand the Best

Students in high-performing urban schools reported that their teachers cared, in part because students perceived that their teachers taught challenging academic content, insisted upon good behavior, and demanded high-quality work. In particular, upper elementary, middle, and high school students offered many examples of their teachers' high expectations as evidence of caring. For instance, at Franklin Towne Charter in Philadelphia, Pennsylvania, students expressed pride in the rigor of the curriculum they were expected to master. "They [teachers] care because they could just give you easy work," one student explained, "but instead they push you to learn tough topics in math, science, and other subjects. When you leave this school, you're ready for college."

Frequently, educators conveyed caring and commitment as they insisted upon scholarly behavior. At Jim Thorpe Fundamental Academy in Santa Ana, California, teachers trained students to behave as scholars. At Bursch Elementary in Compton, California, students knew that they were being prepared to attend college. Their cooperative work groups were named for various colleges and universities. Students were eager to live up to their teachers' high expectations.

At KIPP Adelante in San Diego, California, a middle school student expressed a similar sentiment by stating, "The teachers here want you to have a future. We're going to be able to get into the very best high schools. Our teachers make sure we're learning everything we need to learn." This student and others at KIPP Adelante accepted their teachers' high academic expectations as expressions of caring.

Students also indicated that their teachers' high expectations for their character and behavior was evidence of caring. "The teachers make sure that everybody follows the rules," an Escontrias Elementary (El Paso, Texas) student explained. "There's almost never fights here. This is the safest school I've ever been to. The teachers make sure everybody is safe." At Franklin Towne Charter High School in Philadelphia, Pennsylvania, students expressed the same opinions. "I'm never scared in this building," a female sophomore stated. A male senior reported, "I've been here since my freshman year. I've never seen a fight at school." Students emphasized that teachers, administrators, and support personnel worked hard to make sure they were safe. "You don't have to worry about being picked on or bullied at this school," a student at Cecil Parker Elementary in Mount Vernon, New York, explained. "Teachers make sure that you can do your work and be safe." Students in many of the high-performing schools echoed the belief that their teachers cared enough to create learning environments in which they and all other students were expected to adhere to strong codes of conduct.

Teachers reinforced expectations for positive student behavior by fairly and consistently enforcing reasonable rules. Students were expected to work hard, stay engaged in learning activities, and interact with each other in polite and respectful ways. When students did not follow rules, teachers responded calmly, yet firmly. For example, a teacher at KIPP Adelante quietly and discretely gave her cell phone to a misbehaving student. The student gasped, took the phone, and quietly stepped outside the classroom door. He called his parent, discussed his behavior, and brought the phone back to his teacher. The routine was simple, yet powerfully effective. The teacher did not raise her voice or show any emotion. The teacher did not waste any time with reminders, pleas, or threats.

Consistently, throughout high-performing urban schools, we observed similar firm, fair, and calm enforcement of rules and consequences. A student at Tucker Elementary in Long Beach, California, confessed, "Before I came to this school I used to be in trouble all the time." When asked why things had changed, he explained, "The teachers here care about me. They want me to succeed in school. They like me, but they don't let me get away with anything. This is a good place to be."

Caring Enough to Ensure Success

Just as students perceived that their teachers' high expectations reflected caring, students also believed that their teachers cared enough to ensure they would succeed at meeting those expectations. Students at all grade levels offered detailed descriptions of the efforts their teachers made to help them succeed.

At Lawndale High School near Los Angeles, California, students described how the school's "No D" policy meant they had to work hard. They could not earn credit for courses by barely meeting the requirements for a D grade. They could earn an A, B, C, or a failing grade of F. Students acknowledged that the policy made them work hard; however, they also emphasized that part of the reason they worked so hard was that teachers worked hard to help them succeed. As one Lawndale student stated, "We have great teachers who are always offering tutoring in the mornings and after school or during lunch. They're always there helping us and it's a challenge, but we always get . . . the help we need. It just makes it a great place to be."

Students reported that extra support came from teachers in a variety of ways, including access to additional learning resources (especially technology resources and manipulatives), the presentation of varied examples (especially examples that make it easier for students to relate to concepts), and the availability of additional time. "Sometimes, it's hard for me to understand the science, so my teacher gives me extra time and extra help to make sure my notes make sense," a seventh-grade student at Horace Mann Dual Language Academy in Wichita, Kansas, explained. Similarly, a fourth-grade student at Dreamkeepers Academy in Norfolk, Virginia, reported, "My teacher finds ways to make hard stuff easier. Like she found a CD that made it a lot easier to learn our math." Ultimately, we found that students perceived that their teachers cared enough to believe in their potential to succeed academically. A primary-grade student at Highland Elementary in Silver Spring, Maryland, emphasized, "If you think that you can't do something during class (like you think it's too hard for you), the teachers help you because they know that you can do the work."

It is important to note that teachers at high-performing urban schools do not lower their expectations. They demand effort. At the same time, however, teachers provide a level of support that ensures students will succeed, with reasonable effort. As a result, students feel capable and are willing to risk trying.

Caring Enough to Know and Value Individual Students

A student at Lawndale High School in Los Angeles remarked,

> The teachers here are great. You feel like they're always there for you. You know they're more than just a teacher. They try to get close to you. If you don't understand something, if they see that you're down or there's something wrong, they come up to you and

ask, "What's wrong?" And it's not only a teacher relationship but also someone you can trust.

Students at high-performing urban schools reported that their teachers cared enough to get to know them, to build relationships, and to establish bonds. Teachers maintained a rapport that made them approachable. Teachers demonstrated a genuine interest in their students' ideas, concerns, and aspirations. "My teachers here know my name and greet me whenever they see me," a sophomore at MacArthur High School in Houston, Texas, explained. "They make me feel like I'm somebody." Similarly, a student at Cecil Parker Elementary explained, "When I see my teacher in the hallway or after school, she asks me how my family is doing. She cares about me and she cares about all of us."

At International Elementary in Long Beach, California, one of the teachers established a mentor program. Almost every staff person at the school serves as a mentor to a student. Teachers meet with their mentees weekly and talk about whatever the student wants to discuss. These and similar efforts help ensure that students feel valued.

When parents were interviewed, many emphasized the power of the personal relationships teachers maintained with students. "My daughter would do anything for that teacher," a Golden Empire Elementary (Sacramento, California) parent emphasized. "She [the teacher] has built a bond with my child in just a few months. But, that's like all the teachers here. They just care."

Similarly, a parent at Charles Lunsford Elementary in Rochester, New York, confessed, "Please don't tell anybody, but we moved to a different neighborhood and we're not even supposed to be at this school any more. But, when I tried to suggest to my kids that they would go to a different school, they all had a fit. So I drive across town every day. But it's worth it. These teachers know my kids. They know what makes them tick."

Caring Enough to Model Courtesy and Respect

Teaching styles may vary; however, teachers in high-performing schools demonstrate courtesy and respect in all interactions. As the student at Dandy Middle School in Fort Lauderdale declared (see story at the beginning of this chapter), "They [teachers] give us respect, even when we don't deserve it."

Students (like all individuals) learn to interpret certain actions as demonstrations of courtesy, acknowledgement, or respect. Some actions may be broadly interpreted as disrespectful (e.g., name calling), while other more subtle nuances (e.g., forms of address, methods of correction, eye contact) may signal respect or disrespect within cultural groups. In high-performing urban schools, teachers know their students well enough to know what students interpret as courteous and respectful behavior, and they model such behavior with great consistency.

Students offered a variety of examples to illustrate the ways in which teachers treated them with respect. A junior at Lawndale explained, "If you mess up behavior-wise, they [teachers] don't get weird about it. They stay cool and calm, like they understand you may be going through a rough time. They don't make it worse than it is." A fifth-grade student at Benjamin Franklin Elementary in Bakersfield, California, explained, "If you get something wrong, they tell you that you're wrong, but they don't embarrass you in front of everybody." A fourth-grade student at Golden Empire Elementary in Sacramento, California, commented similarly, "If you don't finish your assignment, the teachers don't yell. They just make you stay in and finish the work."

It is important to note that students reported that their teachers were remarkably consistent in demonstrating courtesy and respect. "At my old school, I had teachers who would act like they cared about you sometimes, then when you did something wrong, they would go off," a Tucker Elementary student explained. "The teachers here are different. They show you respect no matter what you do. It makes you feel like you're special."

Caring Enough to Praise and Acknowledge

In both subtle and overt ways, teachers provide specific, meaningful praise in response to student effort. Because praise is frequent, students (even older students) have become accustomed to receiving praise from their teachers and from each other.

At high-performing urban schools, frequent verbal and written responses from students provide teachers abundant opportunities to acknowledge and praise student efforts. While teachers in these schools are generally positive about their students, they also offer more specific, focused praise. "I like the way you made a logical inference about the character," a third-grade teacher at Horace Mann Elementary in Glendale, California, explained. "Nice explanation of the meaning of slope [in a linear equation]," a Hambrick Middle School (Houston, Texas) math teacher commented.

Most importantly, positive acknowledgement of behavior, effort, and accomplishment was far more abundant in high-performing urban schools than in typical urban schools. While in more typical schools, one might count one or two examples of teachers praising students in a short ten- or fifteen-minute observation, in high-performing schools it was common to observe several such examples in observations of similar length.

In high-performing elementary, middle, and high schools, praise took physical form on the walls of classrooms and hallways. We observed far more examples of recent, high-quality student work in high-performing schools compared to what we found in more typical urban schools. Even in secondary schools, teachers posted outstanding examples of student work.

The posted work represented student efforts across multiple disciplines. In many schools, student writing was featured prominently. Typically, the posted work included positive teacher comments and grades. Often, the work was posted along with the academic objective the assignment was designed to measure. In many cases, teachers also posted a rubric or scoring guide that explained the criteria used to evaluate the assignment.

In some cases, students were eager to show the researchers their work on their classroom walls. "Hey mister, see this. I did this," a student at Bonham Elementary (Dallas, Texas) bragged. Students saw their work on school walls as an indication that they belonged and that they were successful.

Caring Enough to Create Attractive Physical Environments

Posting high-quality student work is one way teachers use the physical environment to create a positive climate for students. More broadly, however, educators in high-performing urban schools make a variety of efforts to use the physical environment to communicate positive regard for students. In particular, classrooms and learning environments are clean, attractive, and well maintained. Students are proud of the places where they learn.

"Look at this school. This doesn't look like a ghetto school," a fifth-grade student at Dreamkeepers Academy insisted. He pointed with pride to the attractive posters, the engaging displays, and the clean floors. Through posters, pictures, and other displays, the physical environment gives students tangible evidence that teachers have high expectations for their immediate and long-term academic success.

What It Is & What It Isn't
Making Students Feel Valued and Capable

■ *What It Is*

Caring enough to demand the best from students

Example: Even though they recognize the next topic on the district's scope and sequence chart as critically important, the middle school math department members acknowledge that it might be impossible to get their sixth-grade students to master the topic in the three days allotted. They determine that approximately 65 percent of their students are two years behind grade level in math. They challenge themselves to determine what students need to know and be able to do in order to master the concept in a way that would meet the grade-level expectation. Then, they determine that they would have a reasonable chance of getting all, or almost all, of their students to this level of mastery if they spent eight days teaching it. Next, they determine the less critical concepts they could remove from "their school's version" of the scope and sequence chart, freeing up the eight days they need to teach this important skill well. Following the eight days of focused instruction, students knew they had accomplished grade-level work. They were proud of themselves. Several expressed that they liked this kind of math. Some talked about how they could be good at math after all.

What It Isn't

Holding students to lower behavioral and academic expectations because of the challenges in their lives

Example: Even though they recognize the next topic on the district's scope and sequence chart as critically important, the middle school math department members acknowledge that it might be impossible to get their sixth-grade students to master the topic in the three days allotted. They determine that approximately 65 percent of their students are two years behind grade level in math, so they decide to focus on a three-day sequence of lessons that would advance the students slightly by teaching the fourth-grade application of the concept. After the three days, some students could be heard complaining about the "baby work" they receive in math. Teachers were frustrated with the students' general lack of mastery. Some students stopped trying. Everyone moved on to the next topic in the scope and sequence.

■ What It Is

Caring enough to ensure students' academic success

Example: The biology teachers notice that most of the students who fail their end-of-course test are students with disabilities. The biology teachers consult with the district's best special educators to identify a set of teaching strategies that should help students with disabilities (as well as other students) master the biology content. They work with the special education teacher at their school to "frontload" key biology vocabulary. In other words, the special education teacher helps introduce the key vocabulary words prior to their introduction in the biology class. Also, with the help of school administrators, the biology teachers organize an after-school biology club, and they encourage the participation of all students, but offer personal invitations to students with disabilities. The club provides practical, fun experiences through which students utilize important biology concepts. After planning this series of actions, the teachers decide how they will monitor the progress of all students, especially students with disabilities, as they work to learn the content on the biology end-of-course test.

What It Isn't

Settling for minimal levels of academic progress

Example: The biology teachers notice that most of the students who fail their end-of-course test are students with disabilities. They decide to use a lower passing score in grading the end-of-course tests for students with disabilities.

■ What It Is

Caring enough to know and value individual students

Example: During passing periods, the art teacher stands at the door and greets students as they walk by. The teacher's quiet, sincere, and personalized greetings and questions help students know that the teacher cares about them individually.

What It Isn't

Missing opportunities to let students know that educators value them individually

Example: During passing periods, the art teacher stands at the door and does not say anything as students pass by, except to tell students to hurry to their next class.

■ What It Is

Caring enough to model courtesy and respect

Example: The fifth-grade teacher asks the students to please turn in their homework. Without warning, one of the students yells out, "Bitch!" The teacher calmly finishes giving directions to the class and then walks back to Mark (the student who made the remark) and whispers for him to follow her into the hall. When the two are in the hallway, the teacher asks, "What was that about?" Mark answers, "I just got a text from my grandmother." Mark shows his cell phone to the teacher, and she sees the text message explaining that Mark's mom was back in jail. "This is the third time she's been in jail," Mark explains with tears rolling down his cheeks. "I'm sorry to hear about your mom," the teacher says. The two of them talk for a minute, and then the teacher asks if Mark needs more time to get himself together. "No. I'm OK," he decides. "So, am I going to have to stay for after-school detention?" Mark asks, before he opens the classroom door. "Absolutely," the teacher responds. "You broke a rule. But, it will be OK. The detention will give you time to work on some math skills."

What It Isn't

Missing opportunities to demonstrate courtesy and respect to students

Example: The fifth-grade teacher asks the students to please turn in their homework. Without warning, one of the students yells out, "Bitch!" The teacher yells back, "If you didn't do your homework, it's your own fault. How dare you call me a name! Get out of my classroom and march yourself down to the office. I don't care if they ever let you come back!"

■ *What It Is*

Caring enough to praise and acknowledge

Example: As the teacher works with seven first-grade students at the reading table, she comments, "I love the way the Princeton group is working quietly together. And I really appreciate the way the Stanford group is following directions. And my San Diego State group, you are reading so well together. What great scholars we have!" Then, the teacher returns her focus to the group at the reading table. Every five minutes or so, she takes the opportunity to notice and comment on the positive things students are doing at their learning centers. Her positive comments seem to fuel their interest in staying on task.

What It Isn't

Missing opportunities to praise and acknowledge

Example: As the teacher works with seven first-grade students at the reading table, she does not notice that the other students are attending to their learning center tasks fairly well. After a while, however, the students are less focused and eventually they become loud and disruptive. The teacher raises her voice to tell students to lower theirs, but that still does not work, so the teacher ends the guided reading lesson early.

■ *What It Is*

Caring enough to create attractive physical environments

Example: The eighth-grade English classes meet in an old portable building on the east end of the campus. Students call the classroom the Writers' Corner because that is the name on the address plaque over the front door. Volunteer students and former students painted the exterior walls with murals of a group of famous artists who represent both genders and various racial/ethnic groups. The same group of volunteers planted sod and flower gardens in ways that make Writers' Corner an attractive place. On one side of the classroom, sofas, love seats, bean bags, and other chairs create the Readers' Circle. On the other end of the classroom, tables and chairs are clustered to facilitate group writing projects. Short bookshelves line the room, filled with a modest collection of interesting reading material. A portable computer lab, with laptop computers, provides easy access to computers and printers. The largest bulletin board in the classroom is the Honor Board. The Honor Board is filled with student writing products that met rigorous criteria. These examples of student work are attractively posted with the scoring guide and teacher comments associated with each project. The contents of the Honor Board are changed each month. Students work hard to ensure that they always have at least one piece of work on the Honor Board. Another wall features the names, pictures, and college affiliations of recent graduates who had been Writers' Corner participants and now attend colleges or universities. A third wall features computer-generated book jackets. When students read books and complete book reports, they generate the book jacket, post it, and sign the inside cover. As other students read the book, they can sign the book jacket, as well. A glass display case holds the self-published books students from the current and previous classes have written. Students can check out, read, and report about these books, just as they can read and report about other volumes in the classroom. Although Writers' Corner is located in a poorly lit corner of the campus, the computer lab has never been the target of vandalism or burglaries.

What It Isn't

Missing opportunities to create attractive physical environments

Example: The eighth-grade English classes meet in an old portable building on the east end of the campus. Students call the classroom the school's ghetto. The exterior walls are dirty and dingy. One window was boarded up two years ago and has never been repaired. Graffiti covers the side of the building closest to the street. The floor of the building is always dirty because students track in dirt and mud from the barren ground between the main building and the portable. Except for a few store-bought posters, the fire drill procedure, and a teacher-made chart with consequences for bad student behavior, the interior classroom walls are bare. The redeeming feature of the building is the relatively large square footage. The teacher has taken advantage of the large space by placing the thirty-five desks into a seven-by-five array with plenty of space in between desks. Most students hate being assigned to classes that meet in the ghetto.

Practice Guide Related to Making Students Feel Valued and Capable

For information on possible uses of this practice guide, please see pages 5–6 in Chapter 1.

1. Was the classroom clean and attractive?   Y   N

2. Were there at least twenty recent (less than one month old) pieces of high-quality student work posted?   Y   N

3. Were there at least fifty recent (less than one month old) pieces of high-quality student work posted?   Y   N

4. Did the teacher demonstrate courtesy and respect in all interactions with students?   Y   N

5. Did the teacher provide specific praise to at least 25 percent of the students?   Y   N

6. To at least 50 percent?   Y   N

7. Did the teacher and students share a rapport that allowed students to ask questions comfortably?   Y   N

8. Did the teacher acknowledge and express appreciation for student effort?   Y   N

9. Did the teacher consistently/fairly enforce rules?   Y   N

10. If off-task behavior occurred, did the teacher redirect it quickly and calmly?   Y   N

In a strong lesson, a "yes" answer is recorded for at least five of these items.
In an outstanding lesson, a "yes" answer is recorded for at least seven of these items.

Suggested Readings Related to Making Students Feel Valued and Capable

Research reveals a significant relationship between students' academic achievement and their perceptions that adults in school care for them. Factors such as school attachment and connectedness, a sense of community, trusting relationships, love and belongingness, and even the quality of school facilities, when combined with teacher support, teacher insistence, and academic press, appear to play a significant role in students' beliefs about themselves as capable learners and, ultimately, their ability to perform academically. The following articles and books further substantiate the major findings from high-performing urban schools presented in this chapter.

Blum, R. W. (2005). A case for school connectedness. *Educational Leadership, 67*(7), 16–20.

    School connectedness has been defined as students' belief that adults and peers in school care about their learning, as well as about them as individuals. Previous studies demonstrated that a connected school environment is related to higher levels of student achievement. Blum convened key researchers, as well as representatives from the government, education, and health sectors, to identify the current state of knowledge related to school connectedness. This article presents a set of research-based principles regarding school connectedness to guide the work of schools.

Bondy, E., & Ross, D. D. (2008). The teacher as warm demander. *Educational Leadership, 66*(1), 54–58.

    Warm demanders approach their students with unconditional positive regard, first coming to know their students as individuals and then insisting that they perform to high standards. Bondy and Ross describe the ways in which warm demanders build relationships deliberately, communicate expectations of success, and support positive behavior.

Breaux, A., & Whitaker, T. (2012). *Making good teaching great: Everyday strategies for teaching with impact.* Larchmont, NY: Eye On Education.

    Breaux and Whitaker offer a wide array of practical suggestions that can help students feel valued, respected, and appreciated by their teachers. These suggestions include ideas for establishing a sincere, caring environment and getting to know students well.

Hallinan, M. T. (2008). Teacher influences on students' attachment to school. *Sociology of Education, 81*, 271–283.

    Research has shown that students who like school have higher academic achievement and lower incidences of disciplinary actions, absenteeism, truancy, and dropping out than do students who dislike school. This study focused on the role of teachers in shaping students' feelings about school. Findings demonstrate that, as teachers provide social and emotional support to their students, they increase the degree to which their students like school, which, in turn, improves students' academic and social outcomes.

Klem, A. M., & Connell, J. P. (2004). Relationships matter: Linking teacher support to student engagement and achievement. *Journal of School Health, 74*(7), 262–273.

   For students to take advantage of high expectations and more advanced curricula, they need support from the adults with whom they interact in school. Klem and Connell observed a general lack of urgency on the part of educators to provide a personalized learning environment for students, even in the face of growing evidence that such an environment influences student academic performance. This study examined the relative payoff in student engagement associated with varying degrees of improvement in relationships between teachers and students.

Lee, V. E., & Smith, J. B. (1999). Social support and achievement for young adolescents in Chicago: The role of school academic press. *American Education Research Journal, 36*(4), 907–945.

   This study explored the relationship between the social support young adolescents received and their learning in mathematics and reading over the course of a school year. Using hierarchical linear modeling methods, researchers found that, on average, social support is positively but modestly related to learning. Both learning and the relationship between social support and learning are contingent on the academic press, that is, the degree to which teachers and students experience an emphasis on academic excellence and adherence to academic standards at their school.

Noddings, N. (2005). *The challenge to care in schools: An alternative approach to education* (2nd ed.). New York: Teachers College Press.

   In this second edition of her seminal book on the ethic of care as applied within schools, Noddings positions care as central to current debates on standardization, accountability, privatization, and the continuous struggle between traditional and progressive methods of education. She considers how schools might be organized around domains of caring, acknowledging individual students' strengths and cultivating these strengths within an environment of caring, rather than competition.

Osterman, K. F. (2000). Students' need for belonging in the school community. *Review of Educational Research, 70*, 323–367.

   Osterman defines a student's sense of community as a feeling of belongingness within a group. In this article, she reviews the research on students' sense of acceptance within the school community. The findings suggest that students' sense of acceptance influences multiple dimensions of their behavior, even as too many schools adopt organizational practices that neglect, and potentially undermine, students' experience of membership in a supportive community.

Scheurich, J. J. (1998). Highly successful and loving, public elementary schools populated mainly by low-SES children of color: Core beliefs and cultural characteristics. *Urban Education, 33*(4), 451—491.

> Scheurich explores five core beliefs and seven organizational cultural characteristics identified by urban principals as foundational to highly successful urban elementary schools. The author describes a practice-based model, developed by urban principals, operationalizing these beliefs and characteristics.

Tschannen-Moran, M. (2004). *Trust matters: Leadership for successful schools.* San Francisco, CA: Jossey-Bass.

> This book offers educators a practical, hands-on guide for establishing and maintaining a caring environment of trust within their schools. Tschannen-Moran explores the leader's role in fostering high-quality relationships among teachers, students, and parents and examines examples of positive outcomes of trusting school environments.

Uline, C., Tschannen-Moran, M., & Wolsey, T. D. (2009). The walls still speak: The stories occupants tell. *Journal of Educational Administration, 47*, 400–426.

> A growing body of research connects the quality of school facilities to student outcomes, including achievement, behavior, and attitudes about school. Less is known about the mechanisms of these relationships. This study examined the link between school building quality and student outcomes through the mediating influence of school climate. From the data, several broad themes related to building quality emerged as central to this interaction between the school facilities and learning, including movement, aesthetics, play of light, flexible and responsive classrooms, elbow room, and security.

9

Leading Students
to Love Learning

The fourth-grade students waited patiently in their white lab jackets as a teacher gave each small group a real pig heart. The three teachers had brought their students into one classroom as they worked together to teach this lesson that combined objectives related to the circulatory system, metric measurement, and data analysis. Like all lessons at Southside Elementary in Miami, Florida, this one centered upon a physical object (in this case, a pig's heart) that students could touch and manipulate.

"What do remember about how the heart is divided?" one teacher asked, calling upon students to talk with each other and recall their learning from the previous lesson.

"The heart is divided into parts," one student told his teammates.

"Yeah, they're called chambers," another student explained.

"Today, you're going inside the heart to see the chambers," the teacher stated enthusiastically. "But first, we need your team to collect as much data as possible about your pig heart. As scientists, you want to collect specific information that will help you know more about this particular pig heart. What are some kinds of data that you might collect about your pig heart? Talk with your teammates and list some kinds of data."

The students generated a list of ideas, including color, weight, width, length, and circumference, reflecting their prior knowledge from both mathematics and other science lab activities. The teachers then gave each group a lab sheet that required them to collect various observations about their pig heart. The teachers engaged the students in discussions of the metric measurements that would work best to record precise information about their pig hearts. The teachers also got students to discuss how they could make sure their measurements were accurate.

"We have to make sure that the weight scale is at zero when it's empty," one student offered.

"When we make linear measurements, we have to start at zero, and if we're counting the big lines [on the measuring tape], we have to make sure we're counting by the right number," another student explained.

The groups collected, checked, and double checked their measurements and recorded them on their lab sheets. Then, the groups began comparing to determine which heart was biggest, heaviest, longest, and so on. Students generated questions that teachers challenged students to answer.

"So why isn't the heart very red?" one student asked.

"Good question," a teacher responded. "What do you think? Talk about it with your groups."

"Maybe pig hearts aren't the same color as human hearts," one student suggested.

"I think it's because there's other stuff covering the heart," another student suggested.

One student went to the website her class had explored previously and found that fat and tissue surrounded the heart. She shared the information with the class.

"What do you think you'll see when we bisect the heart?" one of the teachers asked. Some of the students guessed that they would see blood. Others predicted they would see valves. Others expected to see chambers. Next, a teacher went to each group and used a sharp knife to cut the heart into two halves.

The students watched in awe.

"Wow, I see the chambers!" a boy exclaimed.

"It looks just like the website!" another noted.

"Does my heart look like this?" another asked.

The teachers directed students back to their lab sheets and asked them to collect more data about the chambers.

> *Southside Elementary Museums Magnet School is in the Miami-Dade County School District in Miami, Florida. The school serves approximately eight hundred students in grades pre-kindergarten through five. The school won the National Excellence in Urban Education Award in 2008.*

■

In high-performing urban schools, students are more likely to master challenging academic content, in part because students learn to love learning. Teachers create learning environments that are interesting and exciting. While not every lesson is as powerful as the heart bisection described at the beginning of this chapter, there are a variety of lesson characteristics that magnify student interest in learning. Certainly, in our observations of high-performing urban schools, we saw few lessons that might be considered dull, monotonous, or overly repetitive. In contrast, students were eager to attend classes. Students were excited about what they were learning. For example, at World of Inquiry School in Rochester, New York, students learned by doing. Students worked with manipulatives, they dissected, they discussed problems with partners, and they used computers to investigate problems. Throughout these high-performing urban schools, students were eager to learn more. A variety of practices contributed to this phenomenon.

Enthusiastic Teaching

Students are more likely to learn when teachers evidence enthusiasm for the content they teach. In high-performing urban schools, we observed teachers who were excited about what they were teaching. While some teachers were energetic, positive, and visibly excited about the content they presented, others were more reserved but remained positive about the content they shared and the students they taught.

Typically, when teachers were not working with small groups of students, we found teachers standing and walking while they taught. Teachers were "up" physically and emotionally in ways that helped students engage in the content being learned. For example, at William Bryant School in Cleveland, Ohio; Uplift Education Peak Prep in Dallas, Texas; Montgomery Elementary in Chula Vista, California; and many other high-performing urban schools, we saw teachers moving among groups of students, listening attentively to student responses, pushing students to think more deeply, helping students relate to concepts, and showing students that learning can be interesting, useful, challenging, and exciting.

At Fallon Park Elementary in Roanoke, Virginia, students spoke passionately about their work building volcanoes, conducting electricity experiments, and completing atom projects. Two girls sang a song they had learned about circumference and radius. Students proudly spoke of the hands-on projects they completed at school. "Teachers let us do experiments," they explained. "Teachers make it fun. My teacher talks in an exciting voice."

In many classrooms teachers conveyed enthusiasm by their pacing of instruction. Often, the pace was brisk. Frequent interactions between teacher and students as well as frequent interactions among students added to a robust pace. One teacher at Signal Hill Elementary in Long Beach, California, explained, "I make sure that my students are exhausted by the end of the day. They work hard all day long. We're constantly moving. And, of course, this means that [by the end of the day] I'm exhausted, too."

Relevance of the Content

In high-performing urban schools, teachers help students understand the importance of the content being taught. As students at Franklin Town Charter High in Philadelphia, Pennsylvania, explained, "Here, we learn things that we will need in college and in life." Students are more likely to love learning when they understand the relevance of the content.

Frequently, when we observed classrooms in these high-performing schools, we interrupted students and asked them what they were learning. When they answered, we followed up by asking why they were learning the content they described. First, it is important to note that typically students explained the lesson objective accurately and often with great detail. Second, it was common for students to share rationale such as, "We're going to need to be able to understand this in order to understand computers or become engineers" or "I need to know this in order to succeed in college" or "This is important because this is a real event that could influence my life."

Teachers took time to explain the relevance of what they were teaching. Teachers helped students understand how the lesson could influence their lives currently or in the near future. For example, an algebra teacher at Hambrick Middle School in Houston, Texas (Aldine District) explained, "If your employer paid you by the hour and gave you a bonus for good work, you might need to use a linear equation to help you make sure that your paycheck was accurate."

In contrast, students rarely indicated that the reason for learning something was simply because "It's going to be on the test." Although teachers were deliberate in ensuring that students learned the content that would be covered on state examinations, they offered students more powerful reasons for engaging and wanting to learn.

Often teachers enhanced student perceptions of relevance by making concepts seem real to students (see Chapter 5). For example, at Mueller Charter School in Chula Vista, California, seventh-grade students spend one day each week at a nature center where they engage in real science activities with real scientists. Those activities help students learn about issues that influence local ecosystems in important ways. In various classrooms throughout the country, we observed students acting out activities related to the three branches of government, using food to solve problems with fractions, writing letters to real people in response to real issues, charting and graphing student preferences and accomplishments, and using a wide array of manipulatives. Teachers helped students understand complex abstract concepts by using concrete objects and examples that were highly relevant to students' lives.

Integration of the Arts, Technology, and Physical Education

In high-performing urban schools, teachers enhanced academic lessons through the use of the arts, technology, and physical education. While teachers focused deliberately on important academic objectives in science, mathematics, English, and social studies, they made learning more interesting and powerful through the use of the arts, technology, and physical education. At schools such as Harriet Tubman in Newark, New Jersey; R.N. Harris Integrated Arts in Durham, North Carolina; and Dreamkeepers Academy in Norfolk, Virginia, the use of drama and music helped students learn important concepts related to history, English, mathematics, and science. Music and dance were important tools for teaching academic concepts at Muller Elementary in Tampa, Florida, and at Escontrias Elementary in El Paso, Texas. Teachers at Charles Lunsford Elementary in Rochester, New York, used physical education activities to reinforce concepts related to Venn diagrams.

At William Cullen Bryant in Cleveland, Ohio, the eighth-grade math teacher showed and engaged students in discussions of artwork by Elsworth Kelly, reflecting on various mathematical concepts represented in the artwork, such as symmetry, dimension, and scale. Then, she asked students to create pieces in a similar style, using up to six different colors. Next, the teacher engaged the students in calculating the ratios of their use of different colors and expressing those ratios with fractions, decimals, and percentages.

At Uplift Education Peak Preparatory High School in Dallas, Texas, the eleventh-grade writing teacher used the work of a graffiti artist (Banksy) to help students understand how rhetorical devices can be used to achieve a specific purpose with an audience. Students learned that just as Banksy used specific devices to lead viewers to think, feel, and react in certain ways, they could use specific rhetorical devices to help their readers think, feel, and react in certain ways.

It is important to note that these schools did not shun the use of art, music, and physical education in a blind rush to pursue better test scores. Instead, they recognized that students were more likely to understand and appreciate challenging academic concepts when they saw those concepts reflected in other disciplines. Thus, we saw several examples of teachers using art to reinforce student understanding of geometric concepts. We saw students gaining a deeper understanding of fractions as they learned to read measures of music. We saw students acting out scenes in which historical events were reenacted.

We observed many uses of technology in the teaching of important academic concepts. Smart Boards and clickers were used abundantly throughout the school day at Ira Harbison Elementary in National City, California. Students at Escontrias Elementary in El Paso used iPods to help them practice reading skills. In many schools, we saw students using the Internet to access information, acquire diverse perspectives, resolve disputes about facts, and visit distant places. It is important to note that teachers structured lessons so that students were manipulating the technology (not simply watching the teacher use the technology). As well, it is important to note that teachers did not pursue the use of technology simply to provide students an experience with technology. Instead, teachers used technology to help students better understand the academic objectives they wanted students to learn. While many of the high-performing schools we visited took advantage of digital technology to help students learn, some high-performing schools had limited access to technology resources.

Student-to-Student Engagement

Barron and Darling-Hammond (2008) report that "collaborative approaches to learning are beneficial for individual and collective knowledge growth" (p. 35). In the award-winning schools we studied, we found that students were learning to love learning as they engaged with each other. Students enjoy interacting with their peers. So, in high-performing urban schools teachers were skillful in providing students structured opportunities to talk with and engage their peers around specific academic objectives. For example, at Montgomery Elementary in Chula Vista, California, teachers frequently structured cooperative learning activities or other activities in which students discussed important academic concepts with their peers. In elementary, middle, and high schools, we saw many examples of teachers structuring conversations that required students to discuss, explain, teach, and debate. At all grade levels, we observed examples of cooperative learning in which students worked in teams to help each other reach deeper understandings of lesson objectives. Typically, in these high-performing urban schools, we heard student voices more than we heard teacher voices. However, classroom environments were not chaotic. Students engaged each other to fulfill a specific purpose. Teachers gave students a reason to collaborate, share their thinking, and learn from each other.

Student-to-student collaboration often created opportunities for students to assume formal and informal leadership roles in the learning process. Even as early as kindergarten, as occurred at C.E. Rose Elementary in Tucson, Arizona, teachers prepared students to assume leadership roles in lessons. Teachers were creative in establishing circumstances that gave many students opportunities to share their strengths and assume leadership roles. As a result, students learned to perceive themselves as academically capable. They learned to love learning.

What It Is & *What It Isn't*
Leading Students to Love Learning

■ *What It Is*

Teaching enthusiastically

Example: The teacher begins a review of metric measurement concepts the fourth graders had learned. "Remind me of times you might need to know something about metric linear measurements." Students quickly give answers that include references to foreign travel, the use of tools, watching the Olympics or other sporting events, repairing a car engine, and so on. "Yes, those are great examples! And, you're going to be ready to do all those things and more, because you know a lot about metric linear measurements." To demonstrate to the students that they had learned a significant amount, the teacher begins asking questions such as, "Which is longer: a centimeter or an inch? Is an inch a little longer or a lot longer than a centimeter? How many centimeters are in an inch? Which tool would be longer: a one-inch wrench or a one-centimeter wrench? Which is longer: a yard or a meter? Which race would be longer: a hundred-yard dash or a hundred-meter dash? How much longer? How could you figure it out?" The teacher asks the questions quickly and responds positively whenever students answer correctly. "You are becoming experts in metric linear measurement!" the teacher exclaims. "I'm proud of you. I think you're ready to learn about metric liquid measurements!"

What It Isn't

Teaching without enthusiasm

Example: The teacher begins a review of metric measurement concepts the fourth graders had learned. "Take out a piece of paper. Write your name at the top. I'm going to ask questions that require you to convert metric linear measurements to standard linear measurements. You can use the charts at the front of the room to help you. Ready? Number one: Ten centimeters equals approximately how many inches?" The teacher continues asking nineteen additional similar questions.

■ What It Is

Leading students to perceive the content being presented as relevant

Example: To introduce a unit about the causes of World War II, the teacher engages students in a discussion about the economic difficulties of their community and how some political groups are quick to blame various demographic groups for their economic woes. Using newspaper websites, the students find quotes from various politicians in which they implicitly or explicitly blame certain groups for the nation's, or the community's, economic difficulties. Then, the teacher has students work in groups to read different speeches that Hitler gave in the early 1930s. The groups are asked to identify similarities and differences between the Hitler's rhetoric and the rhetoric of contemporary politicians regarding blame for the economic situation.

What It Isn't

Assuming that students will perceive the relevance of the content being presented

Example: To introduce a unit about the causes of World War II, the teacher presents a lecture on the rise of Hitler in Germany in the 1930s. The lecture describes Hitler's skill at convincing the German people that their economic problems were due to the unfair practices of other European nations and the wealth of Jewish businessmen.

■ *What It Is*

Integrating the arts, technology, and physical education into core academic instruction

Example: The elementary teachers are frustrated about the difficulties they are encountering as they try to get students to learn multiplication facts. The physical education teacher (who participated in the planning meeting) decides that she can help. In the various games she organizes for students, she decides to change the number of points associated with a score. For example, one day a soccer goal might earn eight points to help students practice counting by and multiplying by eight. As students score, she requires them to figure out their point total, counting by the appropriate number and reciting the associated multiplication fact. Students yell, "Eight, sixteen, twenty-four, thirty-two. Eight times four equals thirty-two," as they score for the fourth time.

What It Isn't

Missing opportunities to integrate the arts, technology, and physical education into core academic instruction

Example: The elementary teachers are frustrated about the difficulties they are encountering as they try to get students to learn multiplication facts. They decide that they are doing all they can reasonably do, considering the importance of other math concepts and skills in the curriculum.

■ *What It Is*

Promoting student-to-student interaction

Example: A third-grade teacher introduces the idea that fractions can help describe how a number of objects within a set relates to the entire number of objects in the set. Using a projector, she shows pictures of groups of students in the classroom. The teacher divides the students into five groups. She makes sure that at least one of her most capable mathematicians is in each group. One student serves as the group's recorder. Another serves as the group's accuracy checker. Two of the students are assigned to look particularly at what students in the pictures are wearing or at their physical characteristics. Two focus upon what students in the pictures are doing. The teacher flashes a picture on the screen and each group brainstorms and records as many accurate sentences as possible that describe fractions represented in the picture. They have to do so before the timer bell rings. As soon as the first picture is displayed. Latoya gives her group an answer: "Two-fifths of the kids in the picture are wearing red shirts." "I don't get it," Jerome declares. "How many kids are in the picture?" Latoya asks. "I see five," answers Jerome, thinking maybe it is a trick question. "How many kids are wearing red shirts?" asks Latoya. "Two," Jerome answers with a little more confidence. "Right! Two-fifths of the kids are wearing red shirts. Two out of five," Latoya rushes, while looking at the timer. "Oh, I get it!" Jerome blurts. "Like, four-fifths are wearing socks." "Yes, write it down," Latoya directs, as the group tries to create more sentences.

What It Isn't

Missing opportunities to promote student-to-student interaction

Example: A third-grade teacher introduces the idea that fractions can help describe how a number of objects within a set relates to the entire number of objects in the set. Using a projector, she shows pictures of groups of students in the classroom. The teacher calls upon individual students to create sentences that describe a portion of the students in each snapshot. "Mark, what fraction do you see represented in this picture?" the teacher asks. When Mark does not respond, she calls upon Adriana (who always has her hand raised). "Three-fifths of the students are wearing blue jeans," Adriana asserts correctly. "Yes," the teacher answers, relieved that someone got the answer right. "Who else sees a fraction represented in this picture?" The teacher ignores Latoya (another perennial hand raiser) and calls upon Jerome, but Jerome bites his lip and shrugs his shoulders. "Latoya?" "Two-fifths of the kids in the picture are wearing red shirts," Latoya answers proudly. For the rest of the period, the teacher interacts with Adriana, Latoya, and two other students who seem to understand the concept. Other students sit quietly, seemingly attempting to figure out what all this means.

Practice Guide Related to Leading Students to Love Learning

For information on possible uses of this practice guide, please see pages 5–6 in Chapter 1.

1. Did the teacher probe/delve for student thoughts and opinions?   (Y) (N)

2. Did the teacher demonstrate enthusiasm?   (Y) (N)

3. Did students have choices of activities during the lesson?   (Y) (N)

4. Did students understand the importance of the objective to real-life situations?   (Y) (N)

5. Did the teacher encourage student-to-student conversation concerning the objective?   (Y) (N)

6. Did the teacher provide students leadership opportunities within the lesson?   (Y) (N)

7. Did the teacher integrate content from other disciplines in teaching the lesson objective?   (Y) (N)

8. Did students use technology to help learn the lesson objective?   (Y) (N)

9. Did the teacher allow students to manipulate objects related to the lesson objective?   (Y) (N)

10. Did the teacher engage students in projects/games related to the lesson objective?   (Y) (N)

In a strong lesson, a "yes" answer is recorded for at least five of these items.
In an outstanding lesson, a "yes" answer is recorded for at least seven of these items.

Suggested Readings Related to Leading Students to Love Learning

A significant body of evidence underscores the importance of students' active engagement in, and motivation for, learning. Researchers and scholars have explored the ways in which high-quality instruction influences students' love of learning and willingness to persist. The following articles and books reinforce the major ideas presented in this chapter.

Barron, B., & Darling-Hammond, L. (2008). How can we teach for meaningful learning? In L. Darling-Hammond (Ed.), *Powerful learning: What we know about teaching for understanding* (pp. 11–70). San Francisco, CA: Jossey-Bass.

> Grounded in a focus on teaching for understanding, this book explores how learning environments can become more powerful through the use of inquiry-based learning approaches like project-based or problem-based learning. The chapter provides a wealth of practical, evidence-based approaches for promoting understanding in reading, mathematics, and science.

Certo, J., & Brinda, W. (2011). Bringing literature to life for urban adolescents: Artistic dramatic instruction and live theater. *The Journal of Aesthetic Education, 45*(3), 22–37.

This study examined an innovative literacy/theater program implemented in two sixth-grade classrooms of a high-poverty, urban, western Pennsylvania middle school. The program relied on a partnership with a semiprofessional theater company that produced literature adaptations of young adult novels and designed instructional support materials to meet literacy challenges of reluctant readers, as identified by research and the participating teachers.

Ginsberg, M. B., & Wlodkowski, R. J. (2000). *Creating highly motivating classrooms for ALL students: A schoolwide approach to powerful teaching with diverse learners.* San Francisco, CA: Jossey-Bass.
Ginsberg and Wlodkowski provide a pedagogical framework, along with concrete strategies, for teaching diverse students in ways that tap students' intrinsic motivation, within and across cultural groups.

Guthrie, J. T., & Alvermann, D. E. (Eds.). (1997). *Engaged reading: Process, practices and policy implications.* New York: Teachers College Press.
This volume synthesizes research conducted at the National Reading Research Center (NRRC). Synthesizing investigations on the motivational, social, and cognitive needs of learners, the authors address the qualities and habits of engaged readers; instructional practices that encourage active engagement in reading for elementary, middle, and high school students; the influence of family literacy beliefs and interactions on students as engaged readers; various research methods employed by literacy researchers to study engaged reading; and the implications of this research for literacy-related policies.

Hug, B., Krajcik, J., & Marx, R. (2005). Using innovative learning technologies to promote learning and engagement in an urban science classroom. *Urban Education, 40*(4), 446–472.
Recent reform movements within the United States have called for access to rigorous and authentic science curricula for all students. In light of these reform movements, science educators and policy makers recommend incorporation of learning technologies within science instruction to advance equity and promote learning among diverse learners. This article examines how interactive learning technologies, embedded within an extended project-based science curriculum unit, increases engagement of urban middle school students in actively learning key science concepts.

Kohl, H. (2000). *The discipline of hope.* New York: The New Press.
From his four decades of teaching, Kohl identifies the core principle of the practice, "the discipline of hope," that is the stubborn

refusal to accept limits on what students can learn or what teachers can do by helping students discover the power of their minds.

Marks, H. M. (2000). Student engagement in instructional activity: Patterns in the elementary, middle, and high school years. *American Educational Research Journal, 37*, 153–184.

Studying a national sample of selected schools, chosen because of their significant innovation in students' learning experiences and teachers' professional lives, Marks found considerable variation in student engagement. The research sample included 3,669 students, representing 143 social studies and mathematics classrooms in twenty-four restructuring elementary, middle, and high schools. Specific school factors, such as authentic instructional work and structures of support for learning, proved important in raising student engagement.

Marzano, R. J., & Pickering, D. J. (2011). *The highly engaged classroom.* Bloomington, IN: Marzano Research Laboratory.

Student engagement happens as a result of a teacher's careful planning and execution of specific instructional strategies. This book was designed as a self-study text, summarizing key research and then translating it into recommendations for classroom practice aimed at eliciting high levels of student attention and engagement.

Newmann, F. M. (Ed.). (1992). *Student engagement and achievement in American secondary schools.* New York: Teachers College Press.

Fred Newmann and colleagues present findings from five research projects conducted by the National Center on Effective Secondary Schools, which operated from December 1, 1985, to February 28, 1991. Projects investigated different aspects of engagement and achievement problems through literature reviews, analyses of existing data sets, and new studies of students and staff in thirty-two middle and sixty-two high schools throughout the United States.

Stipek, D. (2002). Good instruction is motivating. In A. Wigfield & J. Eccles (Eds.), *Development of achievement motivation* (pp. 310–330). San Diego, CA: Academic Press.

This book discusses research and theory on how motivation changes as students progress through school, gender differences in motivation, and motivational differences as an aspect of ethnicity. In particular, Stipek's chapter describes research on the relationship between high-quality instruction and student engagement in literacy and mathematics, determining that more conceptual instructional approaches, which incorporated active student participation and opportunities to construct knowledge, were predictive of high levels of student engagement.

Sulla, N. (2011). *Students taking charge: Inside the learner-active, technology-infused classroom.* Larchmont, NY: Eye On Education.

   Sulla offers a compelling, practical vision of a learner-centered classroom in which technology plays a prominent role in advancing student learning. The suggestions offered can help teachers re-conceptualize their classrooms in ways that are more likely to lead students to love learning.

10

Developing Best Practices Throughout a School

Perhaps, the most important lesson to be learned from our studies of high-performing urban schools is that success is attainable. Typical urban schools, with significant challenges, can achieve substantial improvements in teaching that yield remarkable gains in learning. This lesson is important, yet also fairly obvious. An equally important, but somewhat less obvious, lesson relates to the difficulties associated with generating school-wide improvements in teaching. This lesson remains elusive in part because, in these outstanding schools, teachers make their work appear easy. As one watches teachers at Jim Thorpe Fundamental Academy in Santa Ana, California, involve students in gallery walks of their California Missions projects, one does not see the hundreds of hours of professional development and planning that supported teachers' efforts to improve student engagement. As an observer sees teachers at Trinidad Garza Early College High School in Dallas, Texas, prepare students to succeed in college-level courses, the months and years teachers spent coming to know their students, master their content, and establish a college-going culture within their school may not be readily apparent. As a visitor watches teachers at Lauderbach Elementary in Chula Vista, California, engage students in focused conversations, one might mistakenly think that teachers always taught with such an intense focus on specific objectives.

Generating consistent school-wide change in teaching takes substantial time and effort, courage, and risk. In this chapter, we describe why such fundamental change is difficult. As well, we describe how National Excellence in Urban Education Award–winning schools overcame these challenges to implement the high-quality, high-yield teaching practices described in this book.

Challenge 1: People are not likely to change their practice if they don't believe the change will generate worthwhile learning results for their students.

Often, well-intentioned administrators enter schools armed with ambitious goals for improving instructional effectiveness. Almost as often, however, the changes they desire never come to fruition, in part because teachers, counselors, and other frontline personnel do not believe the desired changes are likely to work for their students. These teachers, counselors and frontline personnel are not likely to invest the necessary energy to improve practices if they do not believe the proposed improvements will result in worthwhile outcomes for students.

Even when administrators know and understand the eight teaching practices described in this book, they may not know how to help teachers in their schools believe these practices can work for them. If administrators fail to convince educators these practices have a high likelihood of working in their classrooms, with their students, full implementation may never occur.

This should not be taken as an indictment of teachers. Teachers have good reason to be cynical about the parade of reforms they have been asked to join. Too often, they have been expected to move from one reform to the next, often without substantial evidence of success, without sufficient support for full implementation, and, almost always, without district-level commitment to stay the course.

As we visited high-performing urban schools across the country, we paid particular attention to the strategies principals and other leaders used to move teachers to believe in instructional changes enough to implement them well. In many of these schools, leaders gave teachers extensive opportunities to observe the desired change, so that they might believe in the power of the desired change. For example, several principals organized opportunities for their teachers to examine learning outcomes from a school with similar demographics that was achieving better results. Teachers compiled and examined the data and then visited the higher-performing school. Often, teachers came away thinking, "If they can do this there, we can do even better at our school." And, ultimately they proved themselves correct.

In a similar vein, many leaders provided opportunities for teachers to examine data from their colleagues' students. They then provided opportunities for teachers to visit each other's classrooms and see the practices that were influencing success. When teachers saw that a given teaching practice was workable, doable, and likely to generate better learning results, they were more likely to commit to the hard work necessary to improve their own practices.

It is important to note that teachers are not likely to consider every improvement goal worthwhile. Often, leaders appeal to their teachers to implement new practices because "We need to achieve adequate yearly progress this year" or because "The school board is expecting us to make at least a five-point gain." While these may be worthwhile goals, they may also appear superficial and far removed from the core work of preparing students to succeed in life.

In high-performing urban schools, we observed school leaders who were skillful at helping teachers believe that their efforts would make a difference in the short- and long-term success of their students. For example, a principal might explain, "By achieving adequate yearly progress, we'll help ensure that all of our students, regardless of demographic group, are well prepared to succeed at the next level."

Challenge 2: People are not likely to change their practice if they believe they already implement the requested change.

We have worked with several struggling schools where teachers have received an impressive array of professional development opportunities, spanning many of the teaching practices described in this book. Yet, when noting the lack of implementation of a particular practice, one might hear, "We know all about that practice. We had the training a few years ago, and we've been implementing it ever since. If you didn't see that practice, you must have caught us on a bad day."

The Greek philosopher Epicetus wrote, "It is impossible to begin to learn that which one thinks one already knows." People are not likely to learn to implement a new practice if they inaccurately believe they already implement the practice. Unfortunately, too often educators exit professional development programs with a weak image of the practice they are learning. As a result, there is a human tendency to see the new practice as something they already know and do. Perhaps, with the help of some professional development programs, educators acquire new language for describing their existing professional behavior.

As we engaged with teachers, teacher leaders, and administrators in high-performing urban schools, we found that they worked diligently to help each other create clear, detailed images of the practices they sought to implement. Often working in collaborative teams or professional learning communities, teachers endeavored to create common visions of high-quality implementation of the practice(s) they sought to enact. It is also important to note that educators in these high-performing schools expected themselves to implement practices well, with high levels of fidelity.

Teachers engaged in substantial ongoing dialogue about the practice. Through detailed, regular collaboration, educators talked about what "it should look like" when the practice was done exceptionally well. They talked about what the practice might look like in various types of classrooms in various situations. They tried to differentiate strong implementation from novice implementation. They refused to allow themselves to think they were implementing something well when they were not. In some schools, teachers videotaped each other and reviewed the videotapes to identify examples of strong implementation. In many schools, teachers and administrators worked together to create observation tools and rubrics to help them gauge their own implementation, as well as the implementation of their colleagues.

Challenge 3: People are not likely to change their practice if they perceive that nobody cares or notices if they endeavor to change.

Teachers may not strive to implement new, more effective teaching practices if they perceive that nobody would notice if they made the changes or not. This issue is particularly problematic in typical schools where teaching occurs (literally and figuratively) behind closed doors. When another adult is not likely to walk into a teacher's classroom more than a few times a year; when nobody knows whether or not the teacher is making the effort to improve implementation of an agreed upon practice; when an administrator does not show enough interest to even attend the professional development session, much less check to see if a teacher is attempting to make use of the contents, it is much more difficult to sustain the motivation to try.

In the high-performing schools we visited, progress toward high-quality implementation of effective teaching practices was expected, noticed, discussed, and valued. Often, we asked teachers in the schools how often their principal visited their classroom. Frequently, we heard responses such as, "Practically every day" or "Seems like all the time" or "When she hasn't been by all day, I check to see if something's wrong." And, when principals visited, they often made comments about teachers' progress in implementing the teaching practices that were the focus of the school's professional development efforts.

In some of the high-performing urban schools we studied, it was almost as common for teachers to visit each other's classrooms as it was for administrators to visit. Often members of professional learning communities (e.g., grade-level teams or department teams) visited each other's classrooms. Frequently in these visits, teachers used observation tools or rubrics they helped create. In these schools, the improvement of instructional practice was a high priority. Principals discussed the improvements they were or were not seeing in regular staff meetings. Sometimes, school-wide, grade-level, or department-wide improvement results were discussed, charted, posted, and celebrated. Teachers were likely to commit effort to improve their practice because they knew that improvement was expected and valued.

Challenge 4: People are not likely to change their practice if they perceive they are being asked to change multiple things simultaneously.

In too many schools, teachers feel pressured to change a multitude of practices immediately or sooner. Even when the desired changes are potentially powerful, leaders can dilute improvement efforts by asking teachers to change too many things simultaneously.

An old saying suggests, "If you chase two rabbits, both will escape." Some schools try to chase the whole extended family of rabbits as they pursue multiple good ideas for improving teaching practice. It should come as no surprise that these schools often have few actual improvements in teaching practice and even fewer improvements in student learning results.

The practice of pursuing a different improvement effort every month, semester, or year is almost as unproductive as pursuing multiple improvement efforts simultaneously. Often schools seem to ride the education reform pendulum, swinging from one professional development initiative to the next. Teachers who are eager to improve try to understand and implement proposed changes, but rarely have adequate opportunity to practice, receive constructive feedback, reflect, refine, and try again. At the same time, teachers who are resistant to change have learned that "this too shall pass." They know they can wait quietly and the "reform du jour" will change before anyone expects them to make substantive changes to their teaching practices.

In contrast, at many of the high-performing urban schools we visited, principals and teachers told us they were focused on a very small number of pedagogical improvements. For example, at Lawndale High School near Los Angeles, California, leaders told us that they had been working on checking for understanding for the past two years. Almost all of their professional development efforts had been focused on improving their practice related to this issue.

Just as teachers in high-performing schools focus on helping students master specific content, leaders in high-performing schools focus on helping teachers master specific pedagogical skills. At Signal Hill Elementary in Long Beach, California, teachers told us, "We're pretty much experts at teaching vocabulary." The pursuit of expertise requires focus and persistence.

Challenge 5: People are not likely to change their practice if they perceive that they are likely to fail when they try.

Change involves risk. If a teacher's strategy for addressing a situation has been consistently unproductive, she may be nonetheless reluctant to abandon that strategy, especially if it is the only strategy she knows. Too often, leaders fail to acknowledge the personal and professional risks teachers bear when they attempt to change patterns of professional behavior they have used for years.

Sometimes, overzealous principals push mediocre teachers to resign or transfer when they insist upon immediate improvements in teaching performance. Unfortunately, these principals often have difficulty encouraging replacement teachers to come or stay, because the climate they have created is risk aversive while simultaneously demanding change.

Risk requires trust. Teachers are not likely to extend themselves to try new approaches if they perceive that their leaders or their colleagues are looking for them to fail. In many struggling schools, if a lesson fails, leaders assume that the teacher is incapable of or unwilling to teach well. In high-performing schools, if a lesson fails, leaders are more likely to assume that the teacher needs information, feedback, reflection time, or support. Just as great teachers convince students to take risks because the teacher is committed to helping the students succeed, in high-performing schools, great leaders convince teachers to try challenging, new approaches because the leaders are committed to helping the teachers succeed.

In the high-performing schools we visited, leaders created learning climates within which they did not expect perfection; however, they did expect educators to learn continually from their practice. Effort was essential. Still, when teachers tried new approaches or practices, they were not punished or threatened when those efforts failed. Instead, leaders acknowledged the positive efforts made and helped educators better understand what worked and what did not work and why. Often collaborative teacher groups provided powerful support by sharing ideas, materials, models, and encouragement. The quality of collaborative support helped teachers perceive that changes were feasible.

In many of the high-performing urban schools we visited, there was far greater push for improvement than we observed in struggling schools. But, as Chris Steinhauser, the Long Beach Unified superintendent explained, there was also greater support. The culture of encouragement, support, and teamwork helped teachers feel that these schools were great places to work, even though there were substantial expectations for high teaching quality.

Challenge 6: People are not likely to change their practice if they perceive they do not have the resources, materials, time, training, or support necessary to implement the change successfully.

Support comes in many fashions. Some teachers might think, "I could do this if I could just see someone from my department demonstrate this effectively." Others might think, "I could probably do this well if I had access to the right technology or the right learning manipulatives." Still others might suggest, "I know I could do this well if I had time to plan this with my grade-level team."

Often, in struggling schools, teachers feel their leaders have high expectations for them, but those leaders fail to follow through with critical support. In contrast, in the high-performing schools we studied, leaders had high expectations for their teachers, but they had even higher expectations for themselves. They expected themselves to find, acquire, borrow, construct, or somehow provide whatever teachers needed (and sometimes whatever teachers perceived they needed) in order to implement key improvements successfully. Just as leaders want teachers to have a can-do, no-excuses attitude when it comes to meeting student learning needs, teachers need leaders who have a can-do, no-excuses attitude when it comes to meeting the needs of teachers.

This is, of course, a tall order in a time of budget shortfalls, staff reductions, and cuts in support services. There is nothing easy about providing this caliber of support, even when resources are plentiful. Leaders must be creative, resourceful, persistent, and sometimes even a little rebellious in order to ensure that teachers have the quantity and quality of support they need in order to succeed in improving instruction.

Professional development is often a critical support. However, it should be noted that many teacher workshops and in-service training activities are not particularly "professional" and rarely "develop" anyone's capacity to do anything differently. True professional development must be designed in a way that is likely to help educators make substantive improvements in their professional practice. Real improvements in practice are not likely unless the support is intensive, linked directly to classroom practice, and sustained over time. As described earlier, teachers must have adequate opportunity to practice, receive constructive feedback, reflect, refine, and try again. Initiatives that do not include such support should not be called professional development.

Time often represents the most important support. Teachers need time to plan with their colleagues. They need time to visit other teachers and observe how desired instructional changes look in classrooms like their own. They need the time of their colleagues, so critical friends can observe them, comment, and offer constructive suggestions.

In the high-performing urban schools we studied, leaders worked with teachers and district personnel to find creative ways to provide essential time for planning, collaborating, observing, and providing feedback.

Challenge 7: People find it hard to persist.

If teaching practices could be changed overnight or if school results improved as quickly as the public demanded, the need for persistence would lessen. Unfortunately, the opposite is closer to the truth. Deep change requires time. Substantial, sustainable improvements in learning results take time.

In many urban schools, burnout is an epidemic. Many educators become tired of trying. They find it difficult to keep believing, keep learning, and keep trying when the setbacks and frustrations continue to mount. Bad news floods staff meetings, the teacher's lounge, the morning announcements, the local newspaper, and the school board meeting, washing away whatever resolve might have existed the previous day.

In contrast, in high-performing urban schools, educators persist, often against the same frustrations that overwhelm their colleagues in neighboring schools. They persist because they have learned to work together and support one another. In the face of disenchanting news, they persist because they feel that their colleagues need them. They persist because they perceive they are part of a powerful team that will ultimately succeed in making a difference for students. For example, at Marble Hill High School of International Studies in the Bronx, New York, teachers saw themselves as part of a very exciting team committed to making daily improvements in teaching and learning. Teachers refused to settle for less than the best for themselves and their students.

In high-performing urban schools, educators persist because leaders are skillful at measuring progress and highlighting even the smallest growth. Leaders at these schools understand that almost any shred of data contains successes to be valued, as well as opportunities to improve. Leaders meticulously look for evidence of success and find large and small ways to acknowledge and celebrate improvements.

High-performing schools are not immune to setbacks, disappointments, and frustrations. In our visits to some of these schools, we heard heartbreaking stories of loss. At the same time, however, administrators and teacher leaders nurtured a powerful resiliency in students, in teachers, and in themselves. They helped people believe that they were on the road to excellence. They helped people believe that although the journey was long, the trip was worthwhile for the sake of the students.

Conclusion

Mathematicians relish the notion of existence proofs. If they can find just one example that contradicts a theorem, the existence of the one example proves the theorem inaccurate. The schools we have discussed in this book are existence proofs. They prove false the notion that urban schools serving low-income communities are doomed to low levels of academic achievement.

In this book, we have attempted to capture and describe the salient characteristics of instruction in these schools. We have struggled to do so in a manner that adequately credits the impressive efforts of educators at these schools. Nonetheless, we encourage our readers to see for themselves. Visit these or similar schools, observe their classrooms, talk with their teachers, watch their planning meetings, listen to their problem-solving discussions, and see how they interact with students. Work to build upon our descriptions of their teaching practices in ways that add texture, depth, and meaning.

It is also important to note that while instruction is particularly import-ant at these schools, there are many other important elements at play. For example, within these schools, we see many powerful practices that influ-ence school climate and culture. Educators at these schools are impres-sively adept at creating environments in which students, parents, and other educators feel respected, valued, and appreciated. While this book touched upon some of these issues, there is much more to share that falls beyond the scope of this book.

Similarly, it is important to note that leadership in these schools is a critical topic. While leadership is discussed tangentially throughout the book and more directly in Chapter 10, there is much more to be said about the role leaders play in initiating and sustaining change efforts in high-performing urban schools.

If these high-performing schools stand as existence proofs, then we should share a renewed sense of urgency. These schools prove to us that as a nation, we can do better for our children. Achievement gaps need not exist. As educators, we have the power to positively influence students' lives.

National Excellence in Urban Education 2013 Eligibility Criteria

The National Excellence in Urban Education Award (NEUE) is presented annually to the nation's highest performing urban schools. In May 2013, the National Center for Urban School Transformation (NCUST) will present this award to elementary schools, middle schools, high schools, and alternative schools determined to have the greatest evidence of academic excellence for every demographic group of students they serve. In order to compete for a National Excellence in Urban Education Award, schools must meet or exceed the criteria specified in this document.

General Criteria

1. **Urban Location:** The school must be located in a metropolitan area with a population of 50,000 or more residents. (When in doubt, NCUST checks the U.S. Census Bureau list of Metropolitan Statistical Areas which lists urban areas with a population of 50,000 or more.)

2. **Non-Selective Admissions:** In general, the school may not require students to meet academic criteria in order to attain or retain admission. For example, a school that requires students to possess or maintain a minimum grade point average or pass an entrance test would not be eligible for consideration. In some cases, schools may house programs (e.g., programs for students identified as gifted or talented) that admit children from beyond the school's attendance area through selective admissions. In those cases, schools may be considered for the NEUE award if 1) the percentage of students enrolled through selective admissions is less than 10 percent of the total school enrollment and if 2) the school presents data for this application that excludes all students who were enrolled through selective admissions.

Additionally, schools may not use policies that remove students from enrollment because students fail to meet academic criteria. Schools must indicate the number of students removed from enrollment (by the action of the school/district) throughout the prior year.

3. **Low-Income Eligibility:** Each school must present current and prior year low-income eligibility data. For elementary schools in which the highest grade is grade six or lower, at least 60% of the students enrolled (both in the prior and the current year) must have met federal eligibility criteria for free- or reduced-price lunch. For middle schools in which the highest grade is grade nine or lower, at least 50% of the students must have met the same criteria. In high schools, at least 40% of the students must have met the same criteria.

4. **Adequate Yearly Progress (AYP) Data:** Schools must submit AYP data for the last two years. If schools did not meet all AYP criteria, they must specify which AYP criteria were not met. Unlike prior years, applicants are not required to meet all AYP criteria.

5. **High Rates of Academic Proficiency:** The school must be able to demonstrate that the percentage of students demonstrating proficiency on state assessments, in both 2011 and 2012, is higher than the average of all schools in the state (within the same grade span grouping). For example if across state X, 60% of middle school students demonstrated proficiency in English language arts and 58% demonstrated proficiency in mathematics, a middle school in state X could be eligible to compete for the NEUE Award if 60% or more of their students were proficient in English language arts and 58% or more of their students were proficient in mathematics. The school would need to exceed the state average in at least half of the subject areas/grade levels assessed in 2011 and 2012.

6. **High Rates of Academic Proficiency for Every Racial/Ethnic Group:** The school must indicate the percentage of students who achieved academic proficiency from every racial/ethnic group with at least 20 students who had test scores. The school may be eligible to compete only if, in at least two academic subjects, the percentage of students proficient in each racial/ethnic group exceeds the average of all schools in the state. Using the example above (in item 5), a middle school in state X would be eligible if the percentage of Asian, Black, Latino, Native American, and White students proficient in English language arts exceeded 60% and the percentage of Asian, Black, Latino, Native American, and White students proficient in mathematics exceeded 58%. Each racial/ethnic group must exceed the state average in at least two subject areas in 2011 and 2012.

7. **Evidence of High Achievement for English Learners:** If more than 20 students are identified as English learners, the school must present evidence that a high percentage of English learners are progressing toward proficiency with the English language. As well, the school must present evidence that a high percentage of English learners are achieving greater proficiency in at least two academic subjects. Evidence must include the percentage of English learners demonstrating proficiency on state assessments of English and state academic assessments, but might also include evidence of English learners demonstrating yearly achievement gains on state assessments or other indicators of success.

8. **Evidence of High Achievement for Students with Disabilities:** If more than 20 students are identified as students with disabilities, the school must present evidence that a high percentage of students with disabilities are achieving greater proficiency in at least two academic subjects. Evidence must include the percentage of students with disabilities demonstrating proficiency on state assessments, but might also include evidence of students with disabilities demonstrating year-to-year achievement gains on state assessments or other indicators of success.

9. **Excellence in Science, Technology, Engineering, and Mathematics Education (STEM):** Each school must present evidence that their students are developing strong levels of success in science, technology, engineering, and/or mathematics. This evidence might include the percentage of students demonstrating proficiency on state assessments in mathematics or science. It might also include the percentage of students participating in or completing rigorous classes designed to build knowledge and skills in STEM, the percentage of students participating in extra-curricular activities related to STEM fields, the percentage of students participating in competitions related to STEM fields, the performance of students in STEM-related competitions, or other evidence of accomplishment.

10. **High Attendance Rates:** The school must have evidence to indicate that the average student attendance rate exceeded 92% for each of the past two academic years.

11. **Low Rates of Out-of-School Suspension:** The total number of days students were out of school because of suspensions must be smaller than the total number of students enrolled. For example, if last year, 125 out-of-school suspensions occurred in a school and on average, each suspension lasted two days, this school could be eligible to compete if the school enrolled at least 251 students because there were a total of 250 out-of-school suspension days. Similarly, there must be a low rate of suspension for every

racial/ethnic group of students. For example, if the enrollment of White students was 50, the total number of suspension days for White students would have to be less than 50.

12. **Evidence of Student Success at Subsequent Levels:** Each school applicant must present evidence that their students achieve strong levels of academic success at the subsequent school level (e.g. elementary schools must show evidence that their students are successful at the middle school level; middle schools must show evidence that their students are successful at high school). This evidence might include the percentage of students enrolled in advanced or honors classes, the percentage of students who pass all courses in their first year at the subsequent level, or similar evidence of academic success. Each high school must present evidence that their students achieve strong levels of academic success in college, technical school, or some post-secondary educational environment. This evidence might include the percentage of students who enroll in post-secondary education, the percentage of students who successfully complete the first semester of post-secondary education, or similar evidence of academic success beyond high school.

Additional Criteria for High Schools

In addition to the general criteria, high schools must meet the following criteria:

13. **Percentage of First-Year High School Students Advancing to the Second Year:** Each high school must present the number and percentage of their 2011–2012 first-year students who earned sufficient credit to be promoted to second-year status.

14. **Percentage of Students Earning College Credit or Participating in Advanced Placement Courses during High School:** Each school must present evidence of the number and percentage of students who earned college credit in the prior year. Also, each applicant must present evidence of the number and percentage of students who participated in advanced placement or international baccalaureate courses; the number and percentage who took advanced placement, international baccalaureate, or Cambridge assessments; and the number and percentage who received passing scores.

15. **High Graduation Rates:** Each high school must present the latest four-year adjusted cohort graduation rate (as defined by the U.S. Department of Education). The four-year adjusted cohort

graduation rate must be at least 70% for every racial/ethnic group of students.

16. **Number of Dropouts Recovered:** Each school must present data regarding the number of dropouts they helped re-enter into school. As well, schools must present data indicating the success of recovered students in earning credits and graduating.

Criteria for Alternative Schools

The 2012–2013 school year will be the first year in which NCUST will award alternative schools. Alternative school applicants must meet criteria one through three above. Regarding item two, alternative schools may be considered if they selectively enroll students who have experienced academic and behavioral difficulty in typical schools. Additionally, alternative schools must present data regarding all other criteria (four through 16); however, there are not minimum eligibility criteria associated with these criteria. Alternative schools will be reviewed and considered on a competitive basis.

National Excellence in Urban Education Award Winners

Arizona

C.E. Rose Elementary School, Tucson Unified School District, Tucson, AZ (2012)

California

Benjamin Franklin Elementary School, Bakersfield City School District, Bakersfield, CA (2008)

Lauderbach Elementary School, Chula Vista Elementary School District, Chula Vista, CA (2012)

Montgomery Elementary School, Chula Vista Elementary School District, Chula Vista, CA (2012)

Mueller Charter School, Chula Vista Elementary School District, Chula Vista, CA (2012)

Otay Elementary School, Chula Vista Elementary School District, Chula Vista, CA (2012)

Bursch Elementary, Compton Unified School District, Compton, CA (2009)

Columbus Elementary School, Glendale Unified School District, Glendale, CA (2012)

Horace Mann Elementary School, Glendale Unified School District, Glendale, CA (2010)

Lawndale High School, Centinela Valley Union High School District, Lawndale, CA (2009)

International Elementary School, Long Beach Unified School District, Long Beach, CA (2010)

Signal Hill Elementary School, Long Beach Unified School District, Long Beach, CA (2008)

Thomas Edison Elementary School, Long Beach Unified School District,
    Long Beach, CA (2007)
Tucker Elementary School, Long Beach Unified School District,
    Long Beach, CA (2008)
Lemay Street Elementary School, Los Angeles Unified School District,
    Los Angeles, CA (2010)
Nueva Vista Elementary School, Los Angeles Unified School District,
    Los Angeles, CA (2010)
Montebello Gardens Elementary School, Montebello Unified School
    District, Montebello, CA (2009)
Ira Harbison Elementary School, National School District, National City,
    CA (2009)
National City Middle School, Sweetwater Union High School District,
    National City, CA (2012)
Rancho Cucamonga Middle School, Cucamonga School District, Rancho
    Cucamonga, CA (2007)
Golden Empire Elementary School, Sacramento City Unified School
    District, Sacramento, CA (2009)
KIPP Adelante Preparatory Academy, KIPP Charter, San Diego, CA (2009)
Kearny High School of International Business, San Diego Unified School
    District, San Diego, CA (2009)
Jim Thorpe Fundamental Elementary School, Santa Ana Unified School
    District, Santa Ana, CA (2012)

Florida

William Dandy Middle School, Broward County Public Schools,
    Fort Lauderdale, FL (2008, 2012)
Southside Elementary Museums Magnet School, Miami-Dade County
    Public Schools, Miami, FL (2008)
Muller Elementary Magnet School, Hillsborough County Public Schools,
    Tampa, FL (2006)

Georgia

Charles L. Gideons Elementary School, Atlanta Public Schools, Atlanta,
    GA (2007)
Whitefoord Elementary School, Atlanta Public Schools, Atlanta, GA (2010)

Illinois

Whittier Primary School, Peoria Public Schools, Peoria, IL (2006)

Kansas

Horace Mann Dual Language Magnet School, Wichita Public Schools, Wichita, KS (2010)

Maryland

Highland Elementary School, Montgomery County Public Schools, Silver Spring, MD (2010)

Massachusetts

Community Day Charter Public School, Lawrence Public Schools, Lawrence, MA (2006)

Michigan

Detroit Edison Public School Academy, Detroit, MI (2007)

New Jersey

Branch Brook School, Newark Public Schools, Newark, NJ (2010)
Harriet Tubman Blue Ribbon School, Newark Public Schools, Newark, NJ (2008)

New York

Marble Hill High School for International Studies, District 10, NYC Department of Education, Bronx, NY (2010)
Cecil H. Parker Elementary School, Mount Vernon Public Schools Mount Vernon, NY (2007)
Dr. Charles T. Lunsford School No. 19, Rochester City School District, Rochester, NY (2010)
World of Inquiry School No. 58, Rochester City School District, Rochester, NY (2009)

North Carolina

R.N. Harris Integrated Arts/Core Knowledge Magnet School, Durham Public Schools, Durham, NC (2012)

Ohio

Louisa May Alcott Elementary School, Cleveland Metropolitan School District, Cleveland, OH (2008)

MC2 STEM High School, Cleveland Metropolitan School District, Cleveland, OH (2012)

William Cullen Bryant, Cleveland Metropolitan School District, Cleveland, OH (2012)

Columbus Alternative High School, Columbus Public Schools, Columbus, OH (2007)

Oklahoma

Linwood Elementary School, Oklahoma City Public Schools, Oklahoma City, OK, (2006)

Pennsylvania

Bridesburg Elementary School, School District of Philadelphia, Philadelphia, PA (2008)

Franklin Towne Charter High School, School District of Philadelphia, Philadelphia, PA (2009)

Texas

Dorinda L. Pillow Elementary School, Austin Independent School District, Austin, TX (2007)

Bonham Elementary School, Dallas Independent School District, Dallas, TX (2009)

Nathan Adams Elementary School, Dallas Independent School District, Dallas, TX (2010)

Trinidad Garza Early College High School, Dallas Independent School District, Dallas, TX (2012)

Uplift Education Peak Preparatory High School, Uplift Education Charter Schools, Dallas, TX (2012)

Hambrick Middle School, Aldine Independent School District, Houston, TX (2010)

MacArthur Senior High School, Aldine Independent School District, Houston, TX (2008)

Mary Walke Stephens Elementary School, Aldine Independent School District, Houston, TX (2010)

Escontrias Elementary School, Socorro Independent School District, El Paso, TX (2010)

Virginia

Dreamkeepers Academy at J.J. Roberts Elementary, Norfolk Public
Schools, Norfolk, VA (2008)
Ginter Park Elementary School, Richmond Public Schools, Richmond, VA
(2006)
Thomas H. Henderson Middle School, Richmond Public Schools,
Richmond, VA (2008)
Fallon Park Elementary School, Roanoke City Public Schools, Roanoke,
VA (2009)

References

Barron, B., & Darling-Hammond, L. (2008). How can we teach for meaningful learning? In L. Darling-Hammond (Ed.), *Powerful learning: What we know about teaching for understanding* (pp. 11–70). San Francisco, CA: Jossey-Bass.

Fisher, D., & Frey, N. (2007). *Checking for understanding: Formative assessment techniques for your classroom.* Alexandria, VA: Association for Supervision and Curriculum Development.

Gay, G. (2010). *Culturally responsive teaching: Theory, research, and practice* (2nd ed.). New York: Teachers College Press.

Marzano, R. J. (2007). *The art and science of teaching: A comprehensive framework for effective instruction.* Alexandria, VA: Association for Supervision and Curriculum Development.

Marzano, R. J. (2010). *The art and science of teaching: A comprehensive framework for effective instruction.* Alexandria, VA: Association for Supervision and Curriculum Development.

Marzano, R. J., & Pickering, D. J. (2005). *Building academic vocabulary: Teacher's manual.* Alexandria, VA: Association for Supervision and Curriculum Development.

National Center for Urban School Transformation, The. (2012). San Diego State University. Retrieved from http://ncust.org/wp/.

Scheurich, J. J. (1998). Highly successful and loving, public elementary schools populated mainly by low-SES children of color: Core beliefs and cultural characteristics. *Urban Education, 33*(4), 451–491.

Stiggins, R. (2005). From formative assessment to assessment for learning: A path to success in standards-based schools. *Phi Delta Kappan, 87*(4), 324–328.

Wiggins, G. P., & McTighe, J. (2005). *Understanding by design* (Expanded 2nd ed.). Upper Saddle River, NJ: Pearson Education, Inc.